Contents

Foreword

Judy Wajcman

A S we enter the twenty-first century, it is satisfying to note that the relationship between gender and technology is now an established area of inquiry. Indeed, it has been a significant influence on mainstream social studies of technology which developed during the same period. While technology studies have emphasised the way technological innovations are socially shaped, feminists have demonstrated that gender relations and identities are a vital aspect of the social. As a result of the proliferation in recent decades of feminist research and writing on technology, we now have a much more complex understanding of gender, of technology, and of the mutually constitutive relationship between them. Increasingly, we now work from the basis that neither masculinity, femininity nor technology are fixed, unitary categories but that they contain multiple possibilities and are constructed in relation to each other.

Some of these possibilities are here brought to life in a fresh and innovative way. For the first time, this book seeks to explore individual women's experiences and relationships to technology. While the contemporary women's movement emphasised the value of everyday experience as a basis for knowledge, there have to date been few attempts to draw on this rich source in technology studies. In an exciting new departure, the authors of this volume examine their own relationships to technology using an explicitly autobiographical approach.

Adopting the term 'technobiographies', they bring to bear on technology studies a methodology that has been widely used in gender studies and elsewhere in the social sciences and the humanities. The use of autobiography as a methodology throws new light on women's relationship to technology, bringing into sharp relief the way our experiences are filtered through differences such as race/ethnicity, class, sexuality and generation.

Presenting a diversity of personal narratives like this enables us to transcend once and for all the traditional dichotomy of technology as either empowering or disempowering for women. Instead we see here the many and contradictory meanings, identities and social relations involved. The book is a delight to read and represents a major contribution to understanding the complex ties between gender, technology and subjectivity.

Judy Wajcman is Professor of Sociology, Research School of Social Sciences, Australian National University and Visiting Centennial Professor, Gender Institute, London School of Economics.

Acknowledgements

REFLECTION on the process of writing *Cyborg Lives?* reinforces our awareness of the way in which those lives are enriched by and entwined with others' lives and stories. There are many amongst our friends, families and colleagues and the assorted invisible colleges and professional networks to which we belong who have contributed to the process of producing this book. They have offered, variously, free and frank feedback, helpful suggestions, constructive (and sometimes tactless) criticism, insight into the postmodern condition, magazine articles, succinct critiques unsuitable for a family audience, exotic postcards, unconditional positive regard, administrative assistance, glimpses of the Other, cups of tea and coffee, full English breakfast, help with domestic and digital technologies, theoretical arguments, jokes, moral and financial support, necessary light relief and even, at times, blank incomprehension. Thanks to:

Neena Acharya	Annie Hudson	Libby Tisdell
Alison Adam	Lina Johannson	Alan Tuckett
Rod Allen	David Jones	Robin Usher
Paul Armstrong	Ann Kaloski-Naylor	Tom Valentine
Gerry Bernbaum	Fiona Kennedy	Pete Viney
the late Basil Bernstein	Karen Kennedy	Judy Wajcman
Roger Boshier	Allan Kitson	Guy Wareing
David Boud	Brian Larkin	Linden West
Jim Brown	Ann Lloyd	Dave Willett and his
Rosemary Caffarella	Andy Minnion	cyborg dancing
Ron Cervero	David Morgan	Sue Wise
Pam Coare	Karen Mosman	Butch Wilson
Anne-Marie Ducker	Gill Perkins	Miriam Zukas
Richard Edwards	Gavin Poynter	and to all our fellow
Pete Gartside	Dan Pratt	contributors and
David Gosling	Brian Rix	departmental colleagues.
Budd Hall	Jonathan Rutherford	
Garry Hall	Andrew Sparkes	Flis Henwood
John and Annie Harris	Jackie Stacey	Helen Kennedy
Barbara Harrison	Liz Stanley	Nod Miller
the Henwood-Platzer clan	Pat Staples	*East London, April 2001*

About the contributors

Nanda Bandyopadhyay is a middle-class, middle-aged Indian woman who came to Britain 24 years ago with a Master's degree in solid state physics. She moved over to computer science and, following industrial and teaching careers in pure computing (with some physics and maths), joined the Department of Innovation Studies in 1990.

The hippie trail brought Jules Cassidy to London from Melbourne in 1973. Since then she has edited a book, worked in fringe theatre, become a feminist, supported QPR, watched birds, gone to the opera, failed the cricket test and taken to the academic life.

Flis Henwood's research has, until now, been concerned with understanding the construction of other people's relations to technology, particularly in educational and work settings. Her piece in this collection represents her first attempt to examine her own encounters with technology as well as her first attempt at autobiographical writing.

Gwyneth Hughes's main academic interest has evolved from 'pure' science to science and technology studies over a twenty-year span, with a particular focus on gender/science/technology relations.

Helen Mary Theresa Kennedy is a recovering Catholic.

Linda Leung was born in the Chinese Year of the Boar under the star sign of Gemini and cannot function without her spectacles. Therefore, those who disliked her could legitimately call her a four-eyed, two-faced pig. The suggestion that she has been genetically engineered is not entirely implausible as she regards herself as a hybridised mutant of sorts; she is of Chinese heritage, was born and raised in Australia and has worked in the US and the UK. She now lives in Sydney with her British spouse and their son.

Nod Miller describes herself variously as a professor of innovation studies, an action researcher, a media sociologist, an adult educator, a feminist, a T-group enthusiast, a working-class kid made good, a fashion victim and an ex-hippie.

Sally Wyatt is the daughter of a technologist and a writer, so she writes about technology.

Cyborg lives in context: writing women's technobiographies

Flis Henwood
Gwyneth Hughes
Helen Kennedy
Nod Miller
Sally Wyatt

TECHNOLOGY forms a significant part of all our lives, in the home, at work and at play. We grow up learning about the world through a variety of toys and tools. As adults, many of us find it difficult to imagine a life without washing machines, televisions, cars and computers, technologies that seem to be seamlessly integrated into our lives. Sometimes we might feel frustrated with or critical of technologies which do not fulfil our needs or which we perceive to be destructive. At other times, we might fall in love with the latest state-of-the art technology. Despite the constant presence of technologies, we rarely take the opportunity to reflect fully on our relationships with them.

Cyborg Lives? is a collection of women's accounts of everyday relationships with technology, what we refer to as 'technobiographies'. It is a playful exploration of our technological experiences. At the same time, our stories have serious messages about the social relations of technology and the issues of power that pervade both society and technology. As women, we may be more or less powerless or powerful, and our differences in terms of class, ethnicity, sexuality and occupation inform our technobiographical perspectives.

To explain our novel approach to writing about technology and everyday life, we have employed the now well-known cyborg metaphor, introduced by Donna Haraway in 'A manifesto for cyborgs' (1985). A dynamic synergy, part-human and part-machine, the notion of the cybernetic organism, or 'cyborg', has helped us challenge boundaries not only between the social and the technical and between human and machine, but also between truth and fiction, academic writing and creative writing, insider and outsider, self and 'other'.

In this introductory chapter, we explore the ideas that have informed our work in *Cyborg Lives?* We begin with some background history to the production of *Cyborg Lives?* to set the book in context. We then explore the key themes and approaches informing our work: the cyborg metaphor, the use of autobiography as methodology, and social constructivist approaches to technology. The chapter finishes with a brief review of the individual contributions to the collection.

Cyborg pre-history: the origins of the book in theory and experience

All of the essays in this collection have been written by women who were based in the Department of Innovation Studies at the University of East London at the time of the book's conception. The idea for the book arose during a discussion in June 1996, on one of the Department's annual research 'awaydays'. A group of women were talking about how they had each come to the Department, and someone commented on how richly varied were the backgrounds of those present, with at least six different nationalities represented. The academic disciplines with which colleagues identified ranged from natural sciences to arts. Some present had histories of employment in the computer or communications industries before entering academic life, while others had moved into innovation studies from more conventional, single-discipline departments. Others had entered the Department as mature students, becoming hooked on the eclectic mix of skills and theories characterising its activity, and had graduated to membership of the staff group. Each colleague had come to her present position through a different trajectory, but there was agreement that in each case it seemed logical and fitting that the person concerned had found her way to this unusual educational location.

The Department of Innovation Studies is, as far as we know, unique in British higher education in terms of its name and its combination of activities. Research and teaching focus on the relationship between technology and society. The intellectual underpinnings of this focus are discussed more fully in a later section of this introductory chapter. Courses combine theoretical studies of this relationship with the development of practical skills in the application of information and communication technologies. Central to our work is the unity of practice and theory and the importance of an interdisciplinary approach to the analysis of the technology-society relationship. (See Wyatt, Henwood, Miller and Senker 2000, for a further expression of some of the ideas central to the Department.)

But back to the origins of this book. Those present at the research event exchanged stories about how we had come to the Department. On the cultural island of the awayday, individuals revealed elements of their life histories unfamiliar even to close colleagues. One member of staff remarked on the tendency for each colleague to define herself as marginal in some respect; several colleagues were firmly convinced that their identity was self-evidently less congruent with other members of the Department than everyone else's. We talked about whether this pattern said something significant about technology studies and speculated about how to interpret it. One of us had been engaged in autobiographical exploration for some years, and suggested that a collection of first-person narratives dealing with the relationships of those present to technology would illuminate many theoretical debates and would contrast favourably with drier forms of academic writing. Others agreed, and the project was born.

In the autumn of 1996, a series of meetings began and, by the end of the semester, the technobiographies group was established. The group's task was defined as the collective exploration of personal experience of technology through the use of autobiographical techniques. We coined the term 'technobiography' to describe our enterprise, with this portmanteau word indicating our concern with producing life history narratives that treated relations with technology as a central feature. At one stage it was suggested that techno/auto/biography would more accurately reflect the nature of our work. However, this eight-syllable word was too cumbersome for most of us to manage in speaking or writing, and we settled on the easier to manage 'technobiography' early on. Our preference for the plural form of 'technobiographies' in the group's title reflects pluralist tendencies in the group, and our inclinations towards documenting and celebrating difference rather than similarity.

Membership of the technobiographies group fluctuated somewhat from meeting to meeting, with core membership totalling fourteen. Although women always constituted a large majority (as indeed was the case in the Department of Innovation Studies as a whole), at one stage the group contained several men. Feminist perspectives have been prominent in the evolution of technology studies, and research on gender and technology forms an important strand of the Department's activity, so it was not surprising that a focus on the gendered nature of technological relations emerged early on in the development of the technobiographies group. There were differences of opinion in the group about whether or not having a small minority of male members helped or hindered our work and our understanding of the social relations of technology. While some of the women present felt constrained in what they felt able to discuss freely in a mixed group, none felt inclined to ask the men to leave. Others felt that it was appropriate to have male experience to set against women's experience of technology; some countered with the argument that most of the voices in the literature of technology studies tended to be male. There were spirited discussions about the extent to which an individual story should be seen as representing the experience of any group or category of person, anyway. By the time we entered into negotiations with publishers about getting our stories into print, for one reason or another all of the men had left the group.

In the initial meeting of the group we discussed the form that a technobiographical project might take, and agreed that each member of the group should prepare an autobiographical story to represent some aspect of her or his relationship with technology. At the next meeting, group members took turns to read their stories to the rest of the group, and some common themes were identified. Over the following weeks, we took turns to work on the original stories in pairs and small groups. 'Working on' the stories included: asking questions of, and offering interpretations to, the authors of the narratives; drawing pictures to accompany the written accounts; listing overlapping topics and differences of interpretation; mapping relevant questions and arguments in the emerging literature of autobiography. Certain issues were revisited frequently. 'Is this true?', 'how can you tell if it's true?' and 'does it matter anyway?' were questions which we often asked one another as the project developed. Some colleagues were clear in their belief that autobiographical stories resembled other forms of constructed texts; like films, novels or academic articles, autobiographical stories were just as appropriate for analysis or deconstruction. Others felt that a critique of an autobiographical story could be construed as an attack on the author's personal qualities and social context. Over the years during which we have been engaged in this project, we have all become more readily accustomed to responding to others' comments on our reports of hitherto private histories and personal secrets. However, to the end, there remain differences in the group regarding the possibility of uncovering 'truth' in autobiographical stories. A disagreement about the degree and style of editorial intervention in first-person accounts of experience resulted in one member of the technobiographies group leaving the project at a very late stage, to the regret of the editorial team.

The collective nature of the work undertaken in the technobiographies group, despite its tensions, has been an important aspect of our methodology. Much of our understanding has emerged out of a process similar to that of the consciousness-raising groups of the 1970s. Subsequently, the practice of each contributor reading others' writing and providing feedback has continued throughout the stages of drafting, editing and redrafting.

In one of our meetings we formed sub-groups with shared interests in specific aspects of autobiography. Out of this process developed pairs and groups whose members have co-authored chapters in this book, including the 'Plugs' pair (Cassidy and Wyatt) and the methodologies group (Hughes, Kennedy, Miller and Wyatt, who reflected on and wrote about methodo-logical issues in technobiographies and whose writing forms a central part of this introductory chapter). For some time, we played with the positioning of individuals and groups by means of the metaphor of location 'inside' or 'outside' technology. Some members of the group found this a helpful way of conceptualising changing relations with, and degrees of confidence with, technologies. Others found the suggestion of a binary opposition that seemed to be integral to this device constraining. Relatively late in putting this book together, we decided that reflecting on the metaphor of the cyborg would be a useful focus, a way of synthesising the ideas we were exploring about our often complex and contradictory personal experience of technologies. These ideas are discussed in the next section of this chapter.

What are cyborg lives?

Research on gender and technology now has a long history both within technology studies and within women's studies and gender studies. Feminist studies of technology draw attention to the close relationship between the gendering of technology and the construction of gendered subjectivities. Reviewing the literature in the mid-1990s, Keith Grint and Rosalind Gill argue that, in much of the early research in the field, only 'practices that reinforce or reproduce existing patterns of gender relations were "noticed" analytically' (1995: 17) and that this gave rise to polarised and determinist positions. Technology was either interpreted as oppressive to women or, through its powerful associations, was optimistically assumed to have liberating potential for women and disadvantaged groups more generally. It is in critical response to such essentialist approaches that a new, 'third wave' of feminist technology studies has emerged (Spilker and Sørensen 2000: 270). Central to this third wave has been Donna Haraway's influential article, 'A manifesto for cyborgs' (1985).

One of Haraway's most important contributions to feminist studies of technology has been her insistence that women are not in a position to make an outright refusal of technology central to our feminist projects. Technology is, as she pointed out, fully part of us all, an aspect of our identities. 'The machine is us, our processes, an aspect of our embodiment. We can be responsible for machines; they do not dominate or threaten us. We are responsible for boundaries; we are they' (1985: 99). Her argument is that technology is absolutely central to our everyday lives. Because of this, it is useful to conceive of ourselves as cyborgs, and to use this conceptualisation as a tool for transforming existing power relations, particularly with regard to science and technology. Haraway argues that cyborg imagery can help express two crucial arguments in relation to the politics of science and technology. The first argument is that 'the production of universal, totalizing theory is a major mistake that misses most of reality, probably always, but certainly now' (1985: 100). The second is that:

> taking responsibility for the social relations of science and technology means refusing an anti-science metaphysics, a demonology of technology, and so means embracing the skilful task of reconstructing the boundaries of daily life, in partial connection with others, in communication with all of our parts.   (Haraway 1985: 100)

In this way, Haraway's work has opened up new possibilities for analyses and politics to engage in an up-beat and optimistic exploring the ways in which women's lives are intimately entwined with technologies, albeit in diverse and often very complex and contradictory ways.

It is this challenge that the contributors to this book have taken up through our technobiographical writings. Indeed, technobiographies, we suggest, might be thought of as cyborgian writing. The cyborg metaphor seems particularly well-suited to the practice of autobiographical writing, especially where autobiography focuses on experiences of, or encounters with, technology. Haraway argues that the cyborg is 'a creature of social reality as well as fiction' (1985: 65) and describes her own cyborg essay as 'an argument for pleasure in the confusion of boundaries and for responsibility in their construction' (1985: 66). Thus, she encourages a reflexive approach in writing in much the same way that proponents of autobiography have done. Haraway's words resonate well with those of many of the contributors to this book who speak about, and seek to understand, through their reflexive writings, not only the importance of technology in their own lives, but the importance of the act of writing about their experiences of technology as, in itself, an enabling act in the construction of self-identities.

Haraway's ideas and her cyborg metaphor have been widely adopted in technology studies, cultural studies and gender studies. For example, *The Cyborg Handbook*, edited by Chris Hables Gray (1995), brings together key documents from cyborg history as well as new material which explores the role of cyborgs in space technology, the military, medicine and the imagination. More recently, David Bell and Barbara Kennedy (2000) have produced *The Cybercultures Reader*, which employs the cyborg and related metaphors to explore issues of space, sexuality, bodies and colonisation. In gender studies, too, the cyborg has become a key metaphor for exploring the relations between gender and science/technology in the fields of medicine, bodies, sexuality and reproduction (see, for example, Lykke and Braidotti 1996; Davis-Floyd and Dumit 1998; Wolmark 1999; Kirkup, James, Woodward and Hovenden 2000).

Gill Kirkup (2000) argues that 'Haraway's cyborg ... bridges the language of material feminists working on issues of gender and technoscience, and postmodern feminists working with cultural studies and textual deconstruction' (Kirkup 2000: 5). As a result, the cyborg metaphor has often been put to use by people of very different theoretical and political persuasions. While it seems clear that Haraway intended it to be a political tool with which both to deconstruct the gender relations of technology and to build a new political agenda for feminism, it has more often been employed solely as a tool for deconstruction. It is this latter use to which the metaphor is being put in this collection, for it seems to us that understanding how the gender relations of technology are constituted is a necessary first step for developing new political positions and agendas. The essays in this collection form a small part of that first step.

Nina Lykke (1996) has also employed the cyborg metaphor in her review and critique of feminist studies of science and technology. However, she suggests that feminists should beware the reconstruction of new dichotomies as implied in Haraway's statement that she would 'rather be a cyborg than a goddess' (1985: 101). Since the publication of 'A manifesto for cyborgs', says Lykke, the cyborg (or artefactual) has been preferred by feminists to the goddess (or natural): 'To Donna Haraway and other "cyborg feminists", feminist goddess worship is an expression of a modern nostalgic construction of a "good" (non-existent) origin to return to' (Lykke 1996: 23). Lykke laments the imposition of this new cyborg-goddess binary in feminist studies of science and technology and asks, instead, 'Why not explore the potentials of cybergoddesses?' (Lykke 1996: 28).

The essays in this collection explore the cyborg and goddess concepts in a number of ways that engage with the critiques of Haraway, Lykke and others. We ask how useful it is for us to see ourselves as cyborgs, working as we do in feminist technology studies from backgrounds in arts, humanities, social science and science and technology, contesting the boundary between the technical and the social. However, whilst we have used the cyborg metaphor as a tool in the construction of our techno-biographies, we do not always embrace it wholeheartedly. Like Lykke, some of us are concerned about the new cyborg-goddess binary it imposes; others are concerned to avoid the type of abuse of the metaphor to which Judith Squires (1996) and Irma van der Ploeg and Ineke van Wingerden (1995) have alluded.

Concern about the misuses of the cyborg metaphor are clear in the subtitle of van der Ploeg and van Wingerden's article, 'Celebrating the cyborg? On the fate of a beautiful metaphor in later users' hands' (1995). They express their anxiety about what they describe as the 'intellectual laziness' of later users, who describe the objects of their research as cyborgs but make 'no effort to think through what it adds to call something a cyborg, what such a description might enable us to see, in contrast to other descriptions; in short, what difference it makes' (1995: 399). Their concern seems to be that there is too much deconstruction and not enough feminist reconstruction. Whilst we share their belief in the need for intellectual rigour in the application of the term, we also believe that deconstruction is an important first step in developing new political agendas. Like van der Ploeg and van Wingerden, Squires is critical of the apolitical, euphoric way that the cyborg metaphor has been adopted. Attempting to retrieve the political foundations of the term, she writes that 'whilst there may be potential for an alliance between cyborg imagery and a materialist feminism, this potential has been largely submerged beneath a sea of technophoric cyberdrool.' (Squires 1996: 195).

Many technophoric accounts can, indeed, be found in the literature about women's relationships with technology. For example, some of the contributions in *Wired Women* (Cherny and Weise 1996), a collection of autobiographical essays about women's experiences in cyberspace, promote technology as a source of empowerment. The book contains some first-hand autobiographies, often written in 'cyberspeak', using technical jargon. These cyberfeminists, like Sadie Plant (1997), celebrate a cybernetic future for women but without providing any political justification for their predictions. One of the editors, Elizabeth Reba Weise, describes her initiation into cyberspace that began with the excitement of owning her first computer: 'That night I plugged keyboard to computer to screen and sat down to write. Words poured out of me. My computer felt to me, feels to me still, the way wings must feel to a bird, making flight possible' (1996: viii).

Another contributor, Ellen Ullman, writes on computer love:

I fell in love by email. It was as intense as any other falling in love – no, more so. For this love happened in my substitute body, the one on-line, a body that stays up later, is more playful, more inclined to games of innuendo – all the stuff of romantic love.

(Ullman 1996: 12)

Ullman continues, 'I must stress from the outset there was nothing in this on-line attraction of "sexual harassment" or "environments hostile to women". Neither was it some anonymous, fetishistic internet encounter' (1996: 12). Thus, whilst *Wired Women* represents an important contribution to the mapping of women's experiences of technology and, in its documentation of the pleasures of cyberspace, represents an important counterweight to some of the more pessimistic accounts of women's relationships with technology, it can, at times, appear to border on the technophoric. In contrast, whilst some of the contributions in this present collection do express pleasure in technological encounters, the stories tend to describe rather more ambiguous relationships to technology where both pleasure and danger are understood as situated and contextual.

Thus the abbreviated question *Cyborg Lives?* in the first half of our book's title draws attention to our desire to investigate the extent to which the cyborg metaphor is helpful in understanding our experiences of technologies. Whilst the book makes explicit use of the cyborg metaphor to explore personal relationships with technology, it questions the usefulness of the concept for exploring and explaining these relationships and tries to avoid the worst abuses of the concept outlined by van der Ploeg and van Wingerden and Squires. However, it is important to make clear that whilst some of the strengths and weaknesses of the concept are made visible through the stories we write, this book is not intended as, nor does it represent, a complete and rigorous evaluation of the cyborg metaphor. Rather, we would like the book to be read as an experimental effort at exploring the cyborg metaphor for its potentials and problems in helping us to make sense of our own experiences through the telling of our stories.

Autobiography and its uses

The second half of our book title, *Women's Technobiographies*, points to the first hand, personal accounts of women's relationships to technology contained within the book. We wish these to be read alongside, and as a complement to, the more theoretical literature on gender/technology relations, not as a substitute for that literature. Thus, whilst the book 'speaks to' the theory, it is not a theoretical book. However, by writing our 'techno-biographies', we have attempted to open up a space where the relationship between theory and experience might be explored. Indeed, our project was inspired by the growing interest in autobiographical methods in social science and feminist studies over the last two decades, which have been deployed to explore this relationship.

During this period there has been much debate about what constitutes autobiography with some definitions being so broad as to encompass the types of personal accounts that are central to research methods such as ethnography and oral history (Swindells 1995). Whilst few feminists would dispute the fact that such accounts are crucial in feminist research which seeks to provide a means by which silenced and marginalised voices might be heard, it is less clear why such accounts should be thought of as 'autobiographical' rather than simply 'biographical' or, indeed, personal. The use of the oblique '/' in auto/biography is used in order to acknowledge the close relationship between writing the lives of others in biography and writing one's own life in autobiography. It is also used to signify the nature of each as artful construction (see, for example, Liz Stanley's *The Auto/biographical I* (1992) and the work of the British Sociological Association's Auto/biography Study Group). As mentioned earlier, we decided against the use of the oblique '/' for our own work – techno/auto/biography was considered and rejected by the group as being too clumsy a term. However, we nevertheless subscribe to the view that all biography necessarily includes some autobiographical material (however implicit) and that all autobiography necessarily involves constructing the lives of others as well as of oneself, thus producing both biographical and autobiographical material simultaneously.

One of the major attractions for us in attempting to use autobiography to explore our personal experiences of, and relationships with, technology is that the method facilitates an exploration of the adequacy of much of the theory in the gender and technology field for making sense of our own experiences. Whilst none of us feel technology to be totally alien or oppressive to us, neither do any of us define ourselves as straightforward enthusiasts for technology, confident that we will always shape and control its influence in our lives. Indeed, our varying degrees of perceived agency in shaping technology means that we are interested in mapping out the experiences of technologies lived by members of our group. The autobiographical method seems to provide a useful tool with which we can examine the relationship between our 'lived experiences' of technologies and the categories – such as gender, generation, race, class – commonly used by social scientists when exploring the social relations of technology. Bearing in mind Valerie Walkerdine's argument that such social science categorisation only serves to fragment experience, 'as though we did not live our class, our gender and our race simultaneously' (1989: 206), we determined to see how far the autobiographical method would enable us to explore both the relevance of these categories and their interconnections in our everyday lives.

Our approach clearly raises the now familiar debate in feminism and elsewhere in the social sciences about the value of experience as a basis for knowledge. Autobiography and related methodologies such as 'memory work' are often thought to provide a bridge between theory and experience and, as such, to challenge the separation often found between academic knowledge and everyday experience. For example, Frigga Haug and others (1983) have suggested that by focusing on how social structures are concretely lived by individuals, memory work opens up for exploration the great complexity of the relationship between individuals and social structures. Although these writers acknowledge that individual experience is restricted by social possibilities, they see individuals as 'active agents who are not simply stamped with the imprint of their given social relations' (Haug and others 1983: 25), but who 'construct themselves into existing social relations' (1983: 33). Carolyn Steedman (1987) makes similar observations when she questions the adequacy with which sociological classifications and theoretical frameworks capture personal experience. It is this space, between structure and agency, between theory and experience, which we explore in our technobiographies.

An autobiographical approach also facilitates an exploration of a number of other issues relating to method in social science. These include critiques of methodological notions such as 'objectivity', rejection of the possibility of doing unbiased, value free research and an increasing acceptance that the pretence of researcher neutrality is counterproductive. Feminists have always placed great emphasis on the importance of reflexivity in social research, of researchers acknowledging their place within the research process and of the likely effects of our positionings (Stanley 1990, Hollway 1989, Roberts 1981). The best autobiography should make this practice inevitable and should facilitate the interrogation of positionings, the recognition of partial standpoints and the assumption of accountability, practices that are all central to the cyborg metaphor (Haraway 1985).

Indeed, autobiographers might themselves be thought of as cyborgs. In 'seizing the tools to mark the world that marked them as other' (Haraway

1985: 94), cyborgs construct their own stories and versions of events which are 'fabricated' in a number of meanings of this word. So do autobiographers. For, whilst there is clearly some distinction of content between autobiography, biography and fiction, other differences between these three genres are often assumed. Fiction is seen to be 'made up' and is contrasted with fact, whereas both biography and autobiography are often seen as truth – or at least as representing a search for truth. It is possible to challenge these notions and suggest that autobiography, like biography (and like cyborg stories) has much in common with fiction. A number of contemporary writers argue that the similarities between these genres are greater than is commonly assumed, pointing out that autobiography and biography are as constructed as fiction (see, for example, Miller and Morgan 1993, Stanley 1992).

We also understand autobiographies as constructions in the sense that they are re-presentations of the self for particular audiences at particular historical moments. As one of us has written elsewhere:

> I construct myself through writing [about] myself, as, indeed, I do through my everyday conversations. Much of my social life involves meeting with friends and exchanging accounts and analyses of recent history. I tell stories of what has recently happened to me; often the narratives are tried out with one friend and then honed or edited with another. I am sometimes conscious of working on the characterisation, pace and punchline of a particular narrative. Over time, the issue becomes not so much whether the story is 'true' or 'exaggerated', but rather whether its timing is appropriate and whether the elements are arranged in such a way to maximise drama or ironic effect or to provide a climax or whatever it is I am trying to achieve with or from my audience. In writing the process is more clearly open to scrutiny.
>
> (Miller 1993a: 91)

We suggest that autobiography is also construction in the sense that stories about a past self always involve the act of constructing the past through present concerns, priorities and interests, which helps us to understand our present. The act of remembering is a way of making sense of, and giving meaning to, the present through the use of the past (Clare and Johnson 2000 and Stanley 1992). In this sense, the memories that are presented in autobiography cannot be seen as pure or unadulterated re-presentations of the events of the past. Instead, the events re-told are filtered and interpreted from our perspectives in the present. In the essays that make up this collection, we are concerned with our feelings about, and relationships with, technologies. It is not the case that we have always, or will always, understand our past relations with technology in the ways we describe here. Instead, we interpret past encounters with technology according to our present concerns with it, which are informed not least by the themes of this book. Thus the various layers of construction that operate in the production of autobiographical writing show that the notion of a pure, truthful and authentic autobiography is problematic. To reinforce this point, in the essays that follow, some of the authors aim to make this process of construction visible to the reader.

Our approach to autobiography shares two common features with our approach to the relationship between technological and social change. First, we reject determinist approaches both to narratives of a human life and to narratives of technological change. Second, just as autobiography allows us to take into account many aspects of a person's life rather than reducing people to one or two demographic categories, so our approach to technology emphasises the many issues which need to be considered when attempting to understand both its development and its use. Therefore we now turn to a brief discussion of social constructivism in technology studies and its importance for this project.

Social constructivism in technology studies

A central criticism that technology studies (TS) has levelled at other academic disciplines is that they fail to acknowledge the importance of technology in social relationships and the construction of identity. Indeed the goal of TS might be best understood as making visible both the social character of technology and the constructed nature of the taken-for-granted distinction between the social and the technical. TS rejects a simple materialist definition of technology – that is, 'something that hurts when you drop it on your foot'. While this definition draws attention to the material nature of what most of us consider to be technology – those physical objects such as cars, washing machines and computers – it ignores the 'ology', the knowledge of technics, of tools, of ways of doing things. Technological objects do not come into the world unless there are people who know how to make, design and repair the objects. This is the older, traditional definition of technology – knowledge of the industrial arts. Furthermore, technological objects do not have any value unless people know how to use them. A computer is a rather uninteresting collection of plastic, silicon and metal to those people not familiar with what others skilled in using it can make it do. Thus, as Donald MacKenzie and Judy Wajcman clearly demonstrate in their introduction to the first edition of *The Social Shaping of Technology* (1985), there are at least three levels on which we think about technology: physical objects, the knowledge required to understand and use them, and the knowledge required to create them. In addition, it is also important to pay attention to the symbolic importance of the artefacts themselves: one's choice of CD player, if one can afford to choose, can be as revealing of one's social positioning as the choice of the music to be played on it.

For technology studies, the most interesting questions arise in consideration of the relationship between technology and society. Is society simply the passive recipient of the artefacts created by engineers and designers in remote and isolated laboratories? Our answer to that question is an emphatic 'no'. But there are many ways of arriving at that answer. First, technologists are not some distinct species; they too are part of the society in which they live. Second, technological artefacts are not completely fixed; choices about intended use can be and are made throughout the design process and, beyond this process, in the sphere of consumption, usage is not always as intended. Finally, society is not homogeneous. Different social groups can, and do, have highly varied relationships to the ways in which technology is produced and used. Even within a social group such as 'women', these relationships are varied, as this collection demonstrates.

Cyborg Lives? is heavily informed by these TS principles and assumptions. For too long, social scientists have ignored the study of science and technology, to the detriment of understanding its place in our heterogeneous world. Just as autobiography allows consideration of the intersection of the negotiated, and sometimes conflicting, categories of gender, ethnicity, class and sexuality, so the interdisciplinarity that characterises TS allows exploration of the social, political, economic and cultural dimensions of technology.

Perhaps the closest work to our own comes from that now large body of ethnographic research in technology studies that draws upon biographical accounts to identify and theorise about the 'lived experiences of technology'. Two edited collections which have influenced the work of many of the contributors to *Cyborg Lives?* are *Consuming Technologies: Media and Information in Domestic Spaces* (Silverstone and Hirsch 1992) and *Making Technologies our Own? Domesticating Technology into Everyday Life* (Lie and Sørenson 1996). Both collections report research that draws heavily on personal or biographical accounts of experiences of technology and examine the processes by which technologies are 'appropriated' or 'domesticated' into everyday life. In so doing, the two collections share a common concern: to understand more about the relationship between the material and symbolic aspects of technology and the ways in which technologies are mobilised to construct the meanings, identities and social relations that constitute 'everyday life'.

In feminist technology studies, a significant shift has been made away from both gender essentialism and technological determinism in recent years. In line with constructivist approaches in TS more generally, most feminist technology studies now start from the premise that gender and technology are mutually constitutive of one another (Cockburn and Ormrod 1993; Grint and Gill 1995) and emphasise, in particular, the importance of case studies and detailed empirical study for understanding diversity and specificity in gender-technology relations. In this approach, both technology and gender are understood as 'social achievements' that need to be understood by thorough examination of their mutual construction in specific cultural contexts. Some of the essays in this book build explicitly on this approach.

Another important influence on our essays is the older tradition in feminist studies of technology and science: biographies and autobiographies of women in science and technology. Whilst autobiography is rare in feminist technology studies, biography might be seen as one of the earliest feminist interventions in science and technology studies. Early feminist critics pointed out that women were absent from the histories of science and technology that were built around tales of individual pioneering male scientists. These feminists set out to uncover the lives and struggles of women scientists and technologists who had made significant contributions to their fields. Whilst such biographies might be criticised for their replication of the individual, heroic accounts of scientific and technological developments, they have also made positive contributions to the body of knowledge concerning women's relationships with technologies. Such studies have contributed something more than simply individuals' life stories: they have also added to our understanding both of the gendering of science and technology and of how and why women have been excluded or had their work unrecognised (Rose 1994; Rothschild 1983). For example, the story of Rosalind Franklin and the initial lack of recognition for her contributions to the 'discovery' of DNA alongside James Watson and Francis Crick (Sayre 1975) is now well known. Acknowledgement of women's achievements also inspired Sadie Plant's contribution to the recent 'recovery' of Ada Lovelace as a founder of computing in *Zeros + Ones* (Plant 1997). Opposition to technology is a key theme in the autobiography of Helen Caldicott (1996), an internationally renowned anti-nuclear campaigner, although her account contains little gender analysis. Whether explicitly or implicitly feminist, all of these biographies spotlight individual heroines, and consequently contain little material on the lives of less famous producers of science and technology. The only stories that surface in the public domain present the heroine either as a high priestess of science and technology or as a Cassandra, visionary of an apocalyptic future. In contrast, some of the essays in this collection are written by women who, at some time or another, have thought of ourselves as scientists or technologists, yet who are not sufficiently famous or heroic to be the subjects of biographical texts. We write about the 'becoming' process, about 'taking up' scientist or technologist identities and we reflect on the wider implications of accepting such identities at certain points in our lives.

Biographies and autobiographies of eminent scientists and technologists are examples of the most obvious forms of autobiographical material to be found in the technology studies literature. Another type of autobiographical material is the illustrative or paradigm case of the place of technology in society, such as Wiebe Bijker's almost first-hand account of the 1989 Interstate 880 earthquake in California (Bijker 1993). Bijker uses this example to demonstrate both how completely people take technical systems like roads for granted and how misguided they are to do so. Similarly, Susan Leigh Star (1991) exposes her allergy to onions in her discussion of McDonalds and standardisation specifically and exclusion from socio-technical ensembles more generally: her allergy prevents her from taking a job at McDonalds and often makes it difficult for her even to order a hamburger. Autobiographical material is used briefly by David Edge in his account of the development of Science and Technology Studies as a discipline (Edge 1995). Autobiographical accounts are also the basis for Women Working Worldwide's collection *Common Interests: Women Organising in Global Electronics*, which aims to tell 'in workers' own words, of what it is like to be a woman working on the microelectronics industry's global assembly line' (1991: 13).

Anthropological use of autobiography can also be found in the TS literature, as can the use of autobiography as a rhetorical device as in Bruno Latour's *Aramis or the Love of Technology* (Latour 1996). Only very occasionally do we find examples of TS literature that set out explicitly with the aim of employing autobiographical methodologies, although Sharon Traweek (1988) and John Law (2000) might be thought of in this way. Law, for example, demonstrates how, in his terms, 'the personal' can be used to demonstrate the ways in which the established disorder of technoscience comes into being. He writes that 'stories, effective stories, perform themselves into the material world – yes, in the form of social relations, but also in the form of machines, architectural arrangements, bodies, and all the rest' (Law 2000: 1). Similarly, Skúli Sigurdsson has used autobiographical material in 'Electric memories and progressive forgetting' (1997). Here, he describes his attempt to write a celebration of the 50th anniversary of the Icelandic Association of Electric Utilities and the generational differences in approaches to modernisation and electricity that he experienced in so doing.

Despite these few examples, the explicit use of autobiography is still rare in mainstream technology studies and, perhaps surprisingly, also in gender and technology studies. Furthermore, just as autobiography has not featured strongly in technology studies, so technology has been relatively absent in autobiographical academic literature to date. (Some of the contributors to *Cyborg Lives?* have developed and published technobiographical work which originated in this project – for example, Kennedy 1999). On the whole, it remains the case that whilst technology studies, gender and technology studies and autobiography as social research now have well established histories, they rarely meet. It is our contention that there is much to be gained from closer interplay between them. In synthesising autobiography and technology studies in our technobiographies, we assume, in the spirit of cyborg consciousness, that boundaries (in this case, those around academic specialities) are permeable and are there to be transgressed. The next section introduces our attempts to do just this through our individual technobiographies and illustrates the ways in which those technobiographies address themes central to the cyborg metaphor.

Our cyborg technobiographies

Cyborg Lives? is organised into three main sections. Each section addresses a number of cyborgian themes dealing with questions of boundaries, boundary making and breaking, and the construction of identities. However, each section reflects different locations in relation to technology and technological identities. The first section, 'Encountering technology: consumption, identity and everyday life', concentrates on specific moments in the consumption of technological artefacts and practices. The authors reflect on such encounters with technology and the significance of these encounters for the construction of identities over time. The second section, 'Becoming technologists: on taking up (and making up) technological identities', includes a set of reflexive accounts from those of us who have, at some time or another, identified as scientists or technologists. The concluding short section of the book, 'Resisting the cyborg life?', contains one contribution in which the author takes perhaps the firmest stance against the use of the cyborg metaphor for understanding her own orientation towards technology.

In 'In/different screening: contesting medical knowledge in an ante-natal setting', Flis Henwood presents an autobiographical account of her encounter with the technology of ante-natal screening, raising questions about the relationship between gender, knowledge and techno-science. Henwood's story suggests that the very particular circumstances regarding the conception of her baby (through self-insemination) led to a temporary reversal of gender/knowledge relations in reproductive science and technology, as she became the producer of authoritative knowledge and the medical profession became consumers of her experiential knowledge. Henwood describes how, during her encounter with this technology, she struggled to avoid being caught up in the dominant 'discourse of maternalism' that is structured around a technocratic/resistant romantic dualism, implying that only pro- or anti-technology positions are possible. She suggests that her attempts to operate beyond the dualism, to adopt what might be thought of as a more 'cyborgian' position, brought her into conflict, not only with the medical profession, but also with herself as she continued to be seduced by a technology that she knew could offer no certainties. She argues that her story illustrates some of the very real difficulties women face in being asked to take responsibilities for assessing risk in the ante-natal context and that its themes have wider implications for the emerging new orthodoxy in feminist technology studies which promote cyborgian positionings and practices.

Linda Leung writes about representations of Chinese-ness in film, television and on the Web in 'From set menu to all-you-can-eat: comparing representations of my ethnicity in broadcast and new media technologies'. Her recollections lead her to conclude that the range of images offered in the traditional media of Australia, Britain and the US have not been able to reflect the hybridity and diversity of her ethnicity. She subsequently turns to newer media technologies such as the Internet to seek images of Western Chinese-ness. In exploring the extent of the Chinese diaspora on the World Wide Web, there is no destination for Leung, only detours through some startling and bizarre terrain. With cyborgian playfulness, she seeks and finds on the web an eclectic mixture of representations of her own identity which are hybrid, mutant, elegant and eccentric and which satisfy her hunger after her disappointing encounters with older media. Leung argues that the World Wide Web allows ethnic minorities 'access to the power to signify' (Haraway 1985: 93), to reclaim and appropriate this technology of representation, and in this sense cyborg politics are articulated in her findings. The image of the cyborg is manifest in the construction of ethnicities on the web, which are diverse, hybrid, paradoxical and resistant to dichotomisation. But while the web can be utilised for potentially progressive political work, as Haraway hoped technologies would be used, it can also be instrumental in what might be called a counter-cyborg politics. The web is as much a space of struggle between ethnicities that want to 'mark the world that marked them as other' (Haraway 1985: 94) and those that wish to reinscribe hierarchical dualisms such as East/West.

The next chapter is a collaboration between Jules Cassidy and Sally Wyatt entitled 'Plugging into the mother country'. In this chapter, two young women arrive in the UK from the colonies in the 1970s and are amazed to find electrical appliances that do not have plugs attached to them. This chapter explores how one of the most mundane and taken-for-granted technological artefacts is used to police the boundaries between England and Empire, between feminists constructed as 'real' and those constructed as 'inadequate' and between useless and working electrical goods. The authors' experiences with plugs illustrate how even mundane technologies are invested with the power to mark some people as outsiders and to divide women along the lines of technical competence. The authors explore some problems with the cyborg metaphor, in particular its emphasis on women's positive relationships with technology and acquisition of technical know-how: for both authors, the inability to wire a plug was experienced as a barrier to becoming either cyborg or goddess.

In 'Growing up in the belly of the beast', Sally Wyatt goes to the heart of one of the most defining and controversial technologies of the twentieth century: nuclear power. She also goes to the heart of family life in her story which is firmly located in the techno-social conditions of the late twentieth century. Wyatt is the daughter of a nuclear engineer, who spoke for the Canadian Nuclear Association in the 1970s, and of a writer, who once wrote a novel about a family in which the husband was a nuclear engineer. Wyatt describes hers as a cyborg family which happily ignored the modernist division between the arts and sciences and which moved easily across boundaries, be they geographical or disciplinary. Wyatt's chapter also alludes to Haraway's claims about the importance of writing for cyborgs, of telling and re-telling stories. For Wyatt, cyborgs exist not only in science fiction but in all fiction, and cyborgs are hybrids not only of animal and machine, but also of text. Thus she interweaves extracts from texts written by her father, her mother and herself to explore her cyborg family's awareness of a world constituted by people and objects, processes and discourses.

The second section of *Cyborg Lives?*, 'Becoming Technologists: on taking up (and making up) technological identities', starts with 'HMTK meets HTML: from technofraud to cyberchick', in which Helen Kennedy tells the story of her encounters with multimedia. She describes her immersion into the world of new digital technologies and her journey from technofraud to cyberchick. Reconstructing her story from a diary kept for the purpose of technobiographical research, she reflects on the importance of gender, subculture and insecurity in her experiences of working in a multimedia environment. She describes her own changing feelings about the multimedia technologies with which she works, as well as describing how others have constructed these same technologies, particularly in terms of masculinity and femininity. She concludes that whilst the cyborg metaphor is a useful tool with which to comprehend the range of relationships between women and technology which co-exist simultaneously, its uses are limited. The binary oppositions of masculine and feminine that are rejected in the cyborg literature remain useful as tools with which to make sense of her experience in the world of multimedia.

In Gwyneth Hughes' reflection on gender and technology in a science laboratory, entitled 'Technology and romance in the laboratory: reflections on being a "normal" scientist', the author has selected a year she spent undertaking postgraduate research in a chemistry laboratory as a focus for technobiographical writing. At the time she kept a diary that documented her relationships both with laboratory technology and with her co-researchers and supervisor. Through reflections on extracts from these youthful accounts of her former self, she constructs an account of a female novice crossing and re-crossing boundaries between, for example, taking pleasure in and feeling alienated from science and technology; acceptance and rejection of heterosexuality; being inside and outside the scientific research community. The story of her development of an uneasy respect for, and a familiar working relationship with, laboratory technologies is intertwined with pursuit of a heterosexual romance with a fellow researcher. This relationship comes to represent her acceptability as a woman scientist and gives her a taste of the symbolic power of technologies inside the laboratory. However, as the romance ends, the fantasy of belonging in the laboratory evaporates, and she places herself as an outsider to 'normal science'. This probe into her past provides a contrast between a previous world where science, technology and social relations were considered to be separate entities, and a present world in which recognising the interrelation between these three is fundamental to her lived identity.

'The past lives of a cyborg: encountering "space invaders" from the 1980s to the 1990s' is Linda Leung's second contribution to *Cyborg Lives?* In this short, humorous chapter, Leung describes two key moments in the development of her technological identity: her struggles to gain access to her brother's techno-toys and her experience of attending a demonstration of a multimedia authoring application. She describes her own resistance to the attempts that others have made, consciously or unconsciously, to exclude her from being an insider to technology. Leung's is a story about using technology as a tool to contest the boundary between inside and outside, to disrupt the association of technology with masculinity and thus to assert her cyborg status.

Nanda Bandyopadhyay's contribution to the collection, 'Technology, tradition and transition: the journey of a middle class Indian woman', draws on her memories of childhood and youth to reflect on middle-class life in urban India during the 1950s and 1960s. Her chapter evaluates technology's shifting influence and significance through decades of changing family and social structures, and the role it played in the empowerment of the author, as a woman at home and abroad. Bandyopadhyay describes her interactions with a number of technologies, traditional and modern, initially in India and then in the UK. She argues that technologies have an important role to play in tradition as well as in modernity. She discusses the role technology played in the formulation of her expectations and how she used technology to survive in India and the UK, both of which she characterises as worlds of contradictions, oppressions and opportunities. Her focus is on the central cyborg theme of boundary-making and boundary-breaking, and on how technology can be used, symbolically and otherwise, both to mark and to transgress the boundary between tradition and modernity.

In the final section of this book, Nod Miller explores her relationships with the changing technologies of the bathroom and of music consumption in 'I'd rather be a goddess than a cyborg: technobiographical tales from drains to divas',. She traces her journey from her upbringing in a working-class home where the plumbing failed to function to her present location in a house with top-of-the-range sanitaryware, and over forty years of rock music consumption from vinyl via audio tape to CD and MTV. She demonstrates the importance of the cool blonde rock goddess in the way she constructs herself in her internal life history narratives. Her story highlights how the relations of class, gender, generation and subculture have helped to shape the technological objects with which she interacts and are at the same time symbolically inscribed on their surfaces and properties. While she acknowledges that she writes in an environment which resembles a cyborg's lair and that the centrality of technologies in her subjectivity could be constructed as cyborgian, she concludes that the female archetype of the goddess more accurately captures her stance on technology than the metaphor of the cyborg.

Cyborg lives and women's technobiographies

In this chapter we have attempted to describe the process by which *Cyborg Lives?* was produced and the ideas which have provided the context within which we locate our work. In particular, we have described how we have brought the cyborg metaphor together with autobiography and constructivist approaches in technology studies to form a new practice which we call 'technobiography'. This reflexive form of writing explores both the importance of technology in everyday life and the importance of the act of writing about experiences of technology as, in itself, an enabling act in the construction of self-identities.

In describing our technobiographical influences and practices, we have aimed to draw attention to the similarities between cyborg lives and women's technobiographies. A cyborg life is one in which responsibility for technology is accepted and in which empowering ways of living with technology are sought. It is a life which embraces the multiplicity of possible relationships between self-identity and the technological objects and processes that are offered up in the contemporary socio-cultural context. It is also a life based on a belief in a practice 'that privileges contestation, deconstruction, passionate construction, webbed connections, and hope for transformation of systems of knowledges and ways of seeing' (Haraway 1991: 191-2).

The contestation, deconstruction and reconstruction that Haraway advocates are achieved primarily through the act of writing. As the contributors to this collection acknowledge, writing is central to the cyborg project. Haraway writes that 'writing is pre-eminently the technology of cyborgs … Cyborg politics is the struggle for language and the struggle against perfect communication, against the one code that translates all meaning perfectly' (1985: 95). Thus, cyborg politics involves accepting responsibility for language and for writing as well as for technology. Both cyborg and technobiographical practices aim to expose the myth of objectivity and recognise, indeed celebrate, the partial standpoints from which techno-stories are told. In its emphasis on telling and re-telling stories, on 'seizing the tools to mark the world that marked them as other' (1985: 94), the cyborg metaphor is, as we hope this collection illustrates, well-suited to the practice of technobiography.

Section 1

Encountering technology: consumption, identity and everyday life

In/different screening: contesting medical knowledge in an antenatal setting

Flis Henwood

THIS story is an account of what happened when, pregnant with my first baby, I chose to accept the offer of antenatal screening by taking 'the triple test'. It could be written as a simple narrative account of my engagement with that particular reproductive technology and the emotional and practical issues that arose for my partner and I when the results were ambiguous, indicating potential genetic abnormalities in the baby. However, as the diary extracts from that time suggest, there is no simple narrative truth to be told here. From the start, there are two distinct voices in dialogue. On the one hand, there is the pregnant woman seeking reassurance from the medical experts that all is OK with her baby; on the other, there is the feminist critic of science and technology who, seeking to prevent the 'black-boxing' of this particular technology, asks questions about its construction and implementation, despite the fact that such questioning leads to the production of less favourable results, causing pain, suffering and loss of confidence in the pregnancy overall.

In the account which follows, I try to give space to both these voices, indicating and analysing when and how they came into play during those few weeks in which I engaged with this technology. Both voices are found in the diary extracts presented in this chapter which are taken from a personal diary written at the time and introduced here in italics. In my story, I reflect on those diary extracts and the voices therein whilst, at the same time, try to give the analysis some narrative context.

New reproductive technologies and the discourse of maternalism

Whilst re-reading some of the feminist literature on the 'New Reproductive Technologies' (NRTs) for this piece, I was struck by the way in which so much of the debate has, yet again, become polarised between those that emphasise essentially neutral technologies and women's choice to use or refuse them, and those that emphasise the social construction of NRTs, tending towards the implication that women are necessarily victimised, objectified and denied agency in the face of such patriarchal technologies. I was struck by the fact that the story I had decided to tell involves something rather different, perhaps something in between these poles or, more preferably, beyond a polarised construction altogether. For in it there is a tale of choice without an acceptance of the neutrality of the technology and of an acceptance of the socially constructed character of the technology without a sense of victimisation or objectification. As I hope the story shows, I always felt very active and engaged with the technology, seeking to understand the process of its construction whilst, at the same time, seeking to influence that process.

Coming across the work of Rayna Rapp on genetic counselling and the amniocentesis test has been immensely important for the construction of my story. Her work fascinates me because her analysis resonates so clearly with my experience of antenatal screening in a way that other analyses completely fail to do. Her insight into the process of the negotiation of meaning that constitutes any new technology and her recognition of the potential for contestation and challenge to medical knowledge and authority have both been particularly useful in helping situate my story in an STS (Science and Technology Studies) context.

Rapp points out that one of the major limitations in the NRTs literature is the absence of material that gives a sense of these technologies as being in the process of production where participants are engaged in constant negotiations regarding how they can best be defined and interpreted. In particular, she bemoans the absence of material on 'the multilayered and contradictory processes by which a new reproductive technology was being produced, a new workforce and patient populations created, or a language articulated to describe the impact of these processes on representations of pregnancy, maternity, children and family life' (1993: 60).

Reading these words gave my story more legitimacy: through the telling of my own story, might I be able to offer some new insights into these complex and often contradictory processes? After all, I intended to write about language and meaning and about how the new reproductive technology with which I was engaged was, in the process of its construction, simultaneously constructing other actors: pregnant women, their babies and their families. However, I wanted to go further: to reflect upon the construction of the self, asking who is the 'I' that experienced this particular technology and how can she best be represented? Certainly, there was, and is, no unified self, no authentic voice, no true version of events to be told here. Negotiation over meanings and interpretations of the technology is presented in this story as being not solely between medical experts and users/patients/pregnant women, but as a much more ubiquitous process that includes conflict and contradiction within the self, too. I wanted to understand more about how medical knowledge can be contested and how medical experts respond to such contestation. However, at the same time, I wanted to understand my own rather contradictory reactions to that medical knowledge and my attempt to both contest that knowledge whilst, at the same time, have it legitimated.

I like to think of my struggle as being an attempt to position myself within what Rapp has termed 'the discourse of maternalism'. Rapp has argued that the discourse of maternalism is unhelpfully polarised around the 'technocratic' and the 'resistant romantic' type, one allied with science, the other with nature. This either/or construction attempts to present women's voices as unified and the experience of pregnancy as universal whereas, in her research, the women with whom she spoke were always 'polyphonic' and the supposed universality of pregnancy was 'continuously undermined by its concrete historical and local embeddedness' (1993: 65-66).

I have written my story with this kind of framework in mind – trying to tease out how my particular circumstances, and those of my family and community, were central to how we approached the pregnancy, the screening and the possibility of having a disabled child. In the story I offer here, I present myself as taking up a 'cyborgian' position in relation to the particular technology under consideration – neither 'technocratic' nor 'resistant romantic' but consciously critical of each and of the dualistic discourse of maternalism in general. However, as my account will illustrate, the maintenance of a cyborgian position was not always easy and, if this position

LIVERPOOL JOHN MOORES UNIVERSITY
LEARNING SERVICES

is to represent the preferred feminist political stance in relation to technology, such difficulties need to be made explicit.

A cyborg story?

The technology with which this story is concerned is 'the triple test', an antenatal screening technology designed to produce a probability ratio for the baby being born with either Down's Syndrome or spina bifida. This particular test involves a blood test performed at 16 weeks of pregnancy which measures the levels of three hormones (alpha foetoprotein-AFP, oestriols and human chorionic gonadotrophin-HCG) from which a probability ratio is calculated. The central technology in the story is the 'dating scan', an ultrasound scan, performed early in pregnancy (at about 14 weeks) to determine the age of the foetus and, therefore, the optimum time for the blood test which would produce these probabilities. The age of the foetus, as determined by this scan, is also used as data in the calculations that produce the probabilities.

Antenatal screening has become routine in pregnancy in the UK, especially for women over 35, although practices vary from region to region and from health authority to health authority. The triple test was designed to be used in conjunction with the amniocentesis test. Where the triple test shows a high risk of Down's Syndrome or spina bifida, it can be followed by the amniocentesis test that produces either a positive or negative result for each of these chromosomal abnormalities. At the time of my story (1992-3), the triple test was still fairly new, just out of its 'research phase'. It was considered an important breakthrough in antenatal screening procedures as it would limit the number of amniocentesis tests that were necessary.

Why do I call my story 'In/different screening'? According to one dictionary definition, indifferent means 'without difference of inclination; unbiased, impartial, disinterested; fair, just, even-handed' (*The Shorter Oxford English Dictionary* 1983: 1057). The analysis that is presented through my story addresses the extent to which this particular technology can be understood as 'indifferent' in this sense. This is certainly how the technology is normally understood. After all, it is presented as providing pregnant women and the medical experts with knowledge about the development of the baby that is literally 'indifferent' to the emotional or corporeal experiences of the pregnant women themselves. Indeed, it seeks to improve on those 'experiential knowledges' by rationalising the process of sizing and ageing the foetus. 'Indifferent screening' can, then, be used to imply a value-free, neutral screening technology, producing a rational, objective, science-based knowledge which is more reliable and more authoritative than the experiential knowledge of pregnant women themselves. It is precisely this indifference which is supposed to provide users with confidence and reassurance about the health and development of their growing babies. At worst, such indifferent procedures can indicate a problem at an early enough stage for women to choose to continue the screening process and, via an amniocentesis test, secure more certain information on the basis of which a termination can then be chosen or refused.

There are, of course, strong dualisms at work in this particular construction of the technology – 'rational' is opposed to 'emotional', 'mind' opposed to 'body' – dualisms which are commonplace in medical scientific discourse (and in Enlightenment discourses generally). However, as constructivist STS has shown, such dualisms do not simply describe or explain science and technology *as they are,* in any 'real' sense, but rather serve as part of the dominant discourse of science and technology which works to obscure the cultural construction of the knowledges, practices and artefacts that constitute modern science and technologies. Thus, in constructivist STS terms, the technology in my story cannot, and should not, be understood as value-free or neutral. Antenatal screening technologies are imbued with a whole set of values and assumptions, particularly about what constitutes 'the normal'. Through the telling of my story, I hope to show how 'the normal woman', 'the normal pregnancy' and 'the normal baby' are constructed within the medico-scientific discourse that supports antenatal screening in ways that are both normative and regulative. I also aim to show how, through my interventions based on my own lived experience of 'difference', these constructions were exposed and contested. I present my story as one in which I attempted to take some responsibility for the ways in which I engaged with the antenatal screening process. I took this responsibility in the spirit of my interpretation of Haraway's preferred cyborgian positioning in relation to technology when she states that 'the machine is us, our processes, an aspect of our embodiment. We can be responsible for machines; they do not dominate or threaten us. We are responsible for their boundaries; we are they' (1985: 99). Thus, throughout the antenatal screening period I describe here, I tried to enact this cyborg positioning. However, as my account below shows, this was a very difficult position to sustain in the face of powerful medical discourses on the one hand and my own emotional needs on the other.

Step 1: The test and its result

diary extract 23/12/92

Today was the scan and Hazel and I saw the baby for the first time – it was truly amazing. I don't think either of us were really prepared for the emotions we were to feel. When the image first came into focus and we saw its head, body, arms and legs wriggling about, it was instant tears for us both. The tension, held in from all the previous scans and losses, was released, tears of relief as well as joy.

Having conceived my baby through self-insemination, I knew exactly when I would be 14 weeks pregnant and booked the 'dating scan'. I thought, at the time, how odd it was to book a dating scan to tell me what I already knew but, as it happened, the scan knew different: I was 13 weeks pregnant, it seemed. Interestingly, though, they booked me in for the blood test about two weeks later when I would be only 15 weeks by their calculations, one week earlier than the ideal time for the test.

The average Down's risk for a woman my age at that time was 1:380. A triple test result with a probability greater than 1:250 was considered 'high risk' (in which case, women were offered an amniocentesis test), any probability lower than this and women are told they are 'low risk', so should not worry and do nothing more. I was given my result at a routine antenatal check-up with the midwife: low risk.

Step 2: Negotiating the result/contesting medical knowledge

What was conveyed and delimited by the term 'low risk' given to me? As Rayna Rapp has written, 'Statistics and medical terminology are genres of communication, not simply neutral vocabularies. Both convey and delimit the quantity and quality of information that a counselor provides'. (1988: 148). Low risk. That should have been the end of the story. However, as I had understood from a midwife friend of mine that I would be given a figure – the actual ratio of probability – I asked. '1:280', came the reply.

Again, that should have been the end of the story but again I spoke: 'Oh, pretty close then'. Here, the midwife, sticking to her script, should have reassured me: 'Yes, but still low risk, so no worries there'. Instead, she faltered: 'Oh, yes, did you want to talk to someone, perhaps the woman at the hospital who does the tests?' 'Oh, OK' I said, not really knowing why. The midwife 'phoned her and put me on.

The technician was very happy to engage in the numbers game with me but was all set to reassure me nonetheless. Out of interest, I asked her why they had stopped telling women the actual probabilities and restricted the feedback to 'high risk' or 'low risk' and she hinted, but didn't actually say, that she doubted most women wanted to know more. More fool me, I did. As a feminist, I was resisting their attempts to 'speak for' all women, to assume we were not interested in statistics, in science. Furthermore, in my role as cyborg, I was critical of their attempts to 'black-box' the technology at this point by obscuring the process by which the 'low risk' result was reached.

At some point in our conversation, the technician asked me how sure I was of my 'dates' (that is, of the date when I conceived). 'Very sure, certain', I said, '14th September' and explained that my baby was conceived, very consciously, through self-insemination and only once in the relevant month. From this point on, everything changed. I was no longer being reassured and told everything was fine. 'Oh, in that case, we may get a different result', she said. 'How so?' said I. 'Because your baby was 14 weeks when you had the scan or, more importantly, 16 weeks when you had the blood test. We calculated for a 15-week foetus'. There was a sense of urgency in her voice when she asked me if I would like her to recalculate with 'my dates'.

I was very torn. I knew I was getting sucked in – I wanted desperately to understand why they were offering me a recalculation and, of course, I wanted to know the outcome of that calculation. I should have walked away. A struggle ensued within me: emotionally, I simply wanted reassurance and was therefore happy to accept their result, but the cyborg in me continued to resist their attempts to black-box this technology. I needed to understand how the results were produced and if it really mattered that the dates they had calculated for were not, in fact, the 'real' dates. By their own logic, I was low risk, wasn't that all I needed to know? I could tell the technician wanted to recalculate. I was hooked. I was to attend the hospital antenatal clinic the next day to talk with her and possibly the consultant, too. 'The consultant?' I was worried. My dates were going to be used to produce a worse outcome, I felt sure.

The next day, I went with my partner to the clinic. We met the technician and discussed the test again. She produced a new result: probability for Down's was now 1:84. I had moved from low risk to high risk overnight and all because I opened my big mouth! I had also moved onto the fast track in genetic screening procedures. I was to see the consultant there and then and discuss having an amniocentesis test that would tell me for sure if I was carrying a baby with Down's Syndrome. The test was highly recommended to all high-risk women, although everyone was careful to say it was my/our choice.

In the consultant's room, another difficult exchange ensued. Try as we might, my partner and I could not convince the consultant that we should not really even be there. The logic of their own technology put me at 1:280 and therefore low risk. Together, we had worked out our argument. Following the logic of the discourse and practice surrounding the use of the dating scan, my dates should have been literally irrelevant to their tests. I should have been sent packing. Either the internal logic of their own technology worked or it didn't. The reliability of the whole test surely depended on their calculations which compared actual with expected hormone levels, at a given age of foetus, as determined by the dating scan. We understood very well that the scan dates were not 'real' and that the scan was not producing 'better' or more accurate knowledge than I was, concerning the actual age of my growing baby. What the data from the scan allowed the medics to do was to establish the size of the foetus, from which they 'read off' the gestational age. End of story. Why, then, had they accepted and then recalculated using 'my dates'?

diary extract 17/1/93
Sunday evening and in the midst of a difficult set of decisions. Reading back on my last entry, it's hard to recall the joy I felt that day I had the scan for the 'dating' part of the triple test. My test result has come out to be very ambiguous and we are left needing to decide: (a) whether to go for amniocentesis and (b) if we do and if it's positive – Down's Syndrome – then will we terminate the pregnancy or go on with it? A nightmare set of decisions.

At the same time as struggling to come to terms with the test results and to make an 'informed choice' concerning my options, I struggled to resist the way in which those options had been reached. My feeling then, and now, as I reconstruct that exchange, is that I was listened to where other women are not. Why? After all, the ultrasound scan is used to 'date' pregnancies precisely because women's dates are considered 'unreliable', although, in fact, and paradoxically, the process of construction of that particular technology involves quite contradictory understandings of women and the reliability of their 'self-knowledge'. The data on which the technology was built was, of course, originally taken from pregnant women themselves. These women provided information about when they conceived, doctors then measured the size of their foetuses and, from these, derived size-gestational age pairings. These pairings, although necessarily built on averages, become 'facts' or 'truths' about the 'normal pregnancy' and are applied in other women's antenatal care as superior to these other women's own knowledges, which are thereby rendered 'unreliable'.

On reflection, and in the reconstruction of my story, the work of Latour, Woolgar and others comes to mind. From them, students of STS have learnt much about the construction of scientific facts and the ways in which scientists forget or deny that construction once those facts have been produced and become established (Latour and Woolgar 1979; Latour 1986). Similarly, I recalled a meeting with Ann Saetnan in Trondheim, Norway in May 1997. Ann told me about her research into the controversies surrounding the use of routine ultrasound scans in pregnancy in Norway as I shared a little of my story with her. It was she who pointed out so clearly the contradictory approach to women in the 'before' and 'after' phases of the establishment of medical expertise in this field. On returning home to the UK, I read Ann's work. She writes of these 'before' and 'after' phases as follows:

[women] are in possession of knowledge and skills which experts seek to acquire: in this ['Before'] phase, the experts must accept the patient's reliability and defend it in the scientific community because it constitutes the reliability of the experts' own research data. 'After', once the expert has constructed his own scientific knowledge, future patients' reliability is discredited.

(Saetnan 1996: 55)

So why was my data not discredited in this way? How did I come to be accepted as a reliable source of data about my pregnancy? Was it something about me and the circumstances surrounding my pregnancy that caused the experts to listen? Reflecting on these questions at the time and again today, I keep returning to the idea that I was somehow considered to be outside the norm and the 'normal woman' and that this, somehow, meant that my data was not automatically discredited. But who is 'normal woman' here and how was I different?

In dominant discourse, gender is, of course, always understood in relational and oppositional terms. 'Normal woman' is defined in relation to, and in opposition to, 'normal man'. Furthermore, woman's difference from man is defined in terms of her ability to reproduce, to conceive and give birth, with the 'naturalness' of this process being emphasised. Indeed, Wittig suggests that, in patriarchal ideology, 'woman' always stands for a normative model of reproductive heterosexuality (Wittig 1997). Here, then, normal woman is heterosexual, a potential mother, who conceives her baby via heterosexual intercourse. Thus, in the dominant discourses surrounding reproduction, both woman and man are assumed to be heterosexually attracted to their opposite or other half, a dualistic construction of both gender and sexuality that is both normative and regulative.

It has always seemed to me that it was the fact that I was pregnant by self-insemination that led to my dates being treated as reliable. How can this be explained? I speculate that women's 'unreliability' in dominant discourse, is linked to the conflation of insemination with sexual intercourse, with body rather than mind, with the emotional rather than the rational and therefore with the unreliable, rather than the reliable. I suggest that as a lesbian, choosing to have a baby via self-insemination, (itself assumed to be an asexual, perhaps even technological, act), I triggered, for the medics, some kind of disruption to the dominant discourse – my pregnancy, and my knowledge about it, being treated as more 'mind' than 'body' and therefore more reliable. I was neither a normal woman, nor was I, therefore, having a normal pregnancy and, in these circumstances, the medics stepped outside of their usual frame of reference and allowed my data in.

Step 3: Genetic counselling or quality control?

The consultant recommended amniocentesis and we discussed the risks associated with that test. I knew very well that there was a risk of miscarriage but that the risk varied by hospital and even by consultant. 'What are *your* figures, then?' I joked. He looked worried but not unduly so. 'Between 1:150 and 1:200', he replied. We were seriously into the numbers game now. If we took my dates, the risk of Down's was greater than the risk of miscarriage from the amnio, suggesting we should take the amnio route. However, if we took their dates (again, I cried, 'surely, we should'), the risk from the amnio would be greater, so I should probably leave well alone.

The discussion about the amnio led, as if inevitably, to a discussion of termination, should the result be 'positive' (that is, if I was carrying a baby with Down's Syndrome). 'We may not want to terminate, even if the result were positive', I offered, tentatively. 'Well, there really wouldn't be any point in the amnio then, would there now', the consultant replied, rather too smugly. We explained that it might be important for us to know and *prepare for* a child with Down's Syndrome and that this might be an OK reason for wanting the amnio but he was seriously perplexed now and way off his own ground.

We chatted for some time with the consultant before he found a way out for himself. He offered me another triple test. 'After all', he said, 'you are just over 16 weeks by scan date now and this is the optimum time for testing'. Yes. Just so. Exactly. Back to 'their dates', 'their technology', 'their scientific tests'. Strangely, I felt reassured. How, I asked myself, despite all my knowledge and scepticism about the 'numbers game' in which we were engaged, could I still be hoping for a 'better result' this time?

The discourse and practice surrounding the use of these antenatal screening technologies embody very clear-cut assumptions about what constitutes a 'normal baby', with Down's Syndrome babies being considered 'different' from this norm, abnormal and, ultimately, disposable. According to this medico-scientific discourse, genetic screening is a neutral technology leading to greater choice for women who, in theory, can choose whether to eliminate defects via termination. However, in my case, the consultant seemed unwilling to go ahead with the amniocentesis tests unless I agreed to a termination if a 'positive' result was found. Here, I am reminded of Rothman's words: 'abortion is an integral part of this new [screening] technology' (Rothman 1986: 4), words that make perfect sense if genetic screening is understood as a form of 'quality control' and thus far from neutral.

In the medico-scientific discourse with which I engaged, a positive result meant a termination of the pregnancy and other meanings or interpretations of such a result were literally silenced. My partner and I attempted to disrupt this discourse by suggesting that we might seek to use the amniocentesis test to know and *accept rather than refuse* difference, to *prepare for, rather than eliminate,* difference. As Rapp has written, 'there is no inevitable bridge between a positive diagnosis and an abortion' and the choice any woman makes to take or reject the amniocentesis test, and to keep or end the pregnancy 'flows from the way that pregnancy is embedded in the totality of her life' (1988: 152-153).

In my own case, the need to know was very strong, but a desire to terminate a baby with Down's Syndrome following a positive result was far from clear. My partner and I, together with the baby's father, discussed our options in the light of our very particular circumstances. Several aspects of our individual and collective identities and experiences were relevant in our decision-making. Our collective position as 'other' or 'different' ourselves was one such factor. As two lesbians and a gay man, I, my partner and the baby's father had all experienced that feeling of being 'different', of 'otherness', and now we were experiencing it in a new context, that of parenting. Although never made to feel inferior by any of the medical professionals we came across, we were, of course, acutely aware that lesbian and gay parents are, in general, considered not merely as different from other parents but as somehow less legitimate, too. It seemed to us that disabled people are similarly perceived. For example, as we discussed together at the time, although lesbians and gay men are not normally considered suitable adoptive parents, occasionally disabled children or children with severe learning difficulties are placed with lesbian or gay parents, as if one somehow 'deserves' the other. Perhaps, then, a sense of belonging to the 'other', of pride in our difference, made us very critical of routine terminations for disability.

In my own case, the fact that I have a nephew with Down's Syndrome meant that I had no fear of this particular difference and that I was well aware that disability took many forms and can be interpreted and experienced in many different ways. At an emotional level, I was also very conscious of the message a choice to terminate a Down's Syndrome baby would send to my sister and her husband regarding the value of their son.

Another deciding factor that affected us all in slightly different ways, was our collective 'previous reproductive history' (Rapp 1998: 55). In the end, fear of miscarriage as a result of the amniocentesis test was probably the deciding factor for us. My partner had previously suffered one miscarriage and one ectopic pregnancy. I had had two early miscarriages. We had simply lost too much already. We had begun to think we were not going to have a child at all and our investment in this particular pregnancy was, therefore, huge. However, in refusing the amniocentesis, we understood very well that with a high risk of Down's, we were also, potentially, refusing to reject an 'abnormal' baby, choosing to welcome into our world a child that would be different in some respects to other children, whilst sharing so many other characteristics and attributes. We also recognised, although were not able to express as eloquently as Rapp has done, that 'the difference between a biologically described organism and a socially integrated child, is, of course, enormous' (1998: 67). Thus, we knew very well that whilst an amniocentesis test can tell you whether or not you will have a child with Down's Syndrome, a positive result can tell you nothing about either the severity of the disability or the way in which that disability will be 'lived' by the child, its family and wider community. Over these issues, we still have choices.

Towards closure?

diary extract 17/1/93
Emotionally, I feel very sure that I do not want any more intervention and the thought of a miscarriage caused by an amnio is obviously horrendous. My dreams are all about protecting the baby from others' clutches ... On the other hand, my intellectual, rational side is well hooked into the numbers game, trying to tease out some certainty from the mass of ambiguities and inconsistencies in there ...
Tomorrow, I'll get the results of another triple test which probably won't help much. I'll also see Ruthie [a close friend] and the baby...

19/1/93
We made our decision without getting the results of the latest triple test as they weren't ready when expected. We went upstairs to see Ruth and the baby. Emotional attachment to my baby and growing doubts about our willingness to terminate a Down's baby, together with support from friends for whatever decision we made, all seemed to push in one direction – against amnio and further unnecessary intervention. My feelings were confirmed,

too, by the first movements of the baby when I woke up yesterday morning. Also, after seeing Ruth's baby daughter and holding her, I couldn't imagine wanting to risk mine.

Felt much calmer and sense of joy and satisfaction at the pregnancy coming back again then, finally, this afternoon, I got a call from the technician with the results of the test. Amazingly, now 1:800 for Down's!!

Although I was very pleased that we made our decision against amniocentesis before the results of the third triple test, I still wonder how I would have felt and how differently I would have written this story had that test result put the probability for Down's even higher again or, as did not happen, my son Jamie had been born with Down's Syndrome.

I realise that this story represents just one necessarily individual account. It is based on my own very personal experience of antenatal screening, which may or may not resonate with other women's experiences. I have chosen to interpret it now, as I reconstruct those events for this book, in the context of a struggle to situate myself in relation to the dominant discourse of maternalism that is structured around a technocratic/resistant romantic dualism, implying that only pro- or anti-technology positions are possible. When I think about how I felt and acted at that time, I can see how easily I became caught up in this discourse, whilst intellectually knowing it to be far from adequate. At the time, I often felt cross with myself for my prevarication, for my ambivalent attitude towards testing and re-testing, and for being so easily seduced by a technology that I knew could offer me no certainties. Now I am easier on myself and prefer to see myself as struggling to position myself somewhere beyond the dualistic discourse, at a place where cyborg positionings can be explored but where full resolution and closure with regard to the conflicts and tensions they confront is never completely possible.

Acknowledgements

Thanks to all those who read and commented upon earlier drafts of this paper and to all those who helped convince me that the story was worth telling. Special thanks to Angie Hart, Helen Kennedy, Rachael Lockey, Nod Miller, and Judy Wajcman. Finally, for moral support and courage throughout, many thanks to my 'pretended family', Hazel Platzer, Chris Storey, Jamie and Lizzie.

From set menu to all-you-can-eat: comparing representations of my ethnicity in broadcast and new media technologies

Linda Leung

I N this chapter, I examine technologies of representation and the representation of my ethnicity, beginning with my 27-year diet of television, to which the World Wide Web has been recently added. The web has enabled me to change my patterns of consumption; where previously there was little evidence of the Chinese diaspora on the menu, there is a now veritable feast. My prayers as an ethnic minority cyborg have been answered.

When Linda Carter starred in Wonder Woman in the 1970s, it did not take much of a leap of my seven year-old imagination to pretend that it was me. After all, the similarities were staggering. Her name was Linda. My name was Linda. She had black hair. I had black hair. And when she was undergoing her explosive spinning transformation from ordinary woman to Wonder Woman, she could easily have been Chinese.

I also had my suspicions about Tin Tin from the Thunderbirds. Surely, she was Chinese. The coincidences, again, were astonishing: black hair, dark eyes; her name, Tin Tin, and my Chinese name, Ting Mai. It wouldn't take an investigation by Charlie Chan to conclude that I was starved of televisual fare which could sustain any confidence in my identity as a female born in Sydney, resident in Britain, whose ancestors originate from southern mainland China but have been scattered between Hong Kong, Macau, the Solomon Islands, Venezuela, the United States and Australia. I wanted to see other cyborgs like myself on TV, so that making the connection between image and reality didn't have to be such a gargantuan conceptual detour.

It wasn't until I entered the academic world, where I learnt to make those quotation mark gestures with my fingers, to use words that cannot be found in dictionaries and to 'problematise', that I realised the tragedy of my wooden childhood role models of Western Chinese hybridity (literally in Tin Tin's case and metaphorically in the case of Linda Carter's award winning acting). But at the same time, I was invited by other learned colleagues to sample the delights of post-structuralism: its arguments about the fluidity and paradoxes of identity; its contention that the problem with highlighting the absence of ethnic minorities in the broadcast media is the problem of defining 'ethnic minority' itself. Subsequently, any attempt at definition is a form of straitjacketing which serves to exclude other facets of one's subjectivity. In other words, it's not what you eat, but how you choose to taste it.

I seemed to be allergic yet addicted to the hopes and dreams provided by television. Watching Australian television was akin to fasting. The broadcast media industry seemed to be attempting to purify itself by undertaking its own form of ethnic cleansing. Australian television brought up almost all its characters 'white and bright', the remaining 'stains' were the minor roles which went to people of colour. In the years that *Neighbours* has been broadcast, there has never been an Aboriginal character. The producers believed they were depicting Australia's ethnic diversity when they cast an actor with dark brown hair. These images of Australianness combined with Crocodile Dundee, Sir Les, Kylie, Jason, Clive, Rolf and Skippy, made me wonder whether the White Australia policy was still in force in the broadcast media. There were no pollutants of the cyborgian kind to disrupt such pristine visions of ethnic purity.

Even now, every time I see a Chinese person on television or in a film, I exclaim 'Look! Quick! A Chinese person!'. Then I lunge for the video recorder to try to capture the rare event. It's a rather pathetic attempt at demonstrating to anyone in the near vicinity the relative invisibility of Chineseness in the Western media despite the extent of the Chinese diaspora. To date, I still haven't filled my first video tape which I have lovingly labelled 'Role models and images which reflect my own hybridised ethnicity'. Excluded from the collection are films and programmes actually made in China, although to some extent, I have kept my hunger at bay with *kung fu* movies which apparently incorporate Hollywood-style action adventure with Cantonese values such as loyalty to and vengeance for family and friends (Lee 1991). But *kung fu* movies are the representational equivalent of a Mars bar: it's a snack which provides instant gratification and won't ruin your appetite, but taken excessively, is hardly the basis of a balanced diet of media consumption. It is difficult to regard the invariably dodgy English translation, subtitling and dubbing of Chinese language films as exemplifying hybrid, diasporic ethnicities. Rather, it is an example of seemingly incongruous cultures, of the ill-fitting and unsynchronised juxtaposition of the supposedly mystic Orient with the cosmopolitan West. This is not the disruption of complacent, unified subjectivities or the upheaval of so-called 'natural' states of being desired by my typically cyborgian weaknesses for crises of identity. Bruce Lee and Jackie Chan's ethnicity is never in question: they are depicted as kosher Chinese.

If Hong Kong martial arts movies can be regarded as the snack equivalent of Western Chinese representations, then my main meals have consisted of the occasional grain of rice. Depictions of Chinese people outside China or Hong Kong are scattered few and far between as seen in:

- Saffy's friend in *Absolutely Fabulous*
- Burt Kwouk, Harry Hill's comedy sidekick on *The Harry Hill Show*
- an episode of the *X-Files* in which members of the Chinese community in San Francisco die in mysterious circumstances
- a cop on *Hawaii Five-O*, one of Jack Lord's junior officers
- a Chinese actor in the US whose career has consisted of playing villains in series like *Murder She Wrote*
- a character in the Levi's Chinese laundry advertisement
- one of the guests at the ambassador's reception in the Ferrero Rocher advertisement.

You can see I start to get desperate towards the end of the list.

Nevertheless, the menu has improved somewhat with time, with two significant and relatively recent representations of Australian-Chineseness. The first of these was a character called Kelly in *Home and Away*, a Chinese Australian girl who moves to Summer Bay with her father (who is never seen, present but absent). She has no history, only serving as a romantic interest and object of rivalry for two of the permanent characters. Once her purpose is served, she moves out of Summer Bay (or rather is driven out by scriptwriters) with no explanation of why her family arrived there in the first place. She does experience some racist name-calling from the school bully but this is only secondary to the main events and implies that prejudice is an individual (rather than structural or institutional) problem.

But the positioning of Kelly as object of desire and sexual attraction enables the possibilities of an inter-racial relationship to be explored rather than avoided as taboo. Also her Australianness is never doubted. Depictions like this are similar to being treated to a posh meal, a special occasion where every moment should be savoured.

My second experience of TV silver service is May in *Heartbreak High*, who has no familial ties at all and is the anarchist amongst the ensemble of protagonists. In one episode, she invites her new boyfriend to her house for dinner, which he assumes will be a Chinese meal. After he finishes his plate of Chinese food, she tells him she didn't cook it and admits that she bought it at the local takeaway. She warns him not to make assumptions about her. He subsequently develops food poisoning, instigating every stereotype possible about lack of hygiene in the kitchens of Chinese restaurants and the backyard slaughter of domestic animals to use in Chinese dishes. Nonetheless, an alternative reading of this would be that May, in being unable to cook, undermines the usual association of Chineseness with culinary expertise in Chinese cuisine. She is not represented as being part of a traditional Chinese extended family, but, rather implausibly for a sixteen year old, lives alone.

In spite of these rare 'binges', I would still conclude that over my 27 years' consumption of broadcast media, television has not been able to capture the nuances of my (or any) ethnicity. It has followed more or less the same recipes for too long, using the same old ingredients. The images I have discussed have been drawn from the mediocre set menus of US, UK and Australian television which have changed in small degrees over the years. Call me fussy about my TV diet but what I really wanted was a banquet of images, new combinations – *à la* cyborg manifesto – never tried before, where you don't know what's coming next and there's so much to choose from that you don't know whether you can fit it all on your plate.

Thus I have more recently been salivating over the new broadcast media technology that is the World Wide Web. Within it is the potential for a feast of texts and images which illustrate the hybridity and diversity of the Chinese diaspora. It can cater for special requests for ethnicity to be represented in ways which avoid exclusion and essentialism for those who have a taste for depictions which undermine traditional ones seen in the broadcast media. I have tested the World Wide Web's capacity to whet and satisfy my appetite for such representations of ethnicity by searching it for sites which articulate and reflect my identity. Using various search engines and only the keywords 'Western Chinese' as my utensils, I have chewed over some delicious and dodgy digital concoctions.

There were some procedural inconsistencies here in that a search for representations of my ethnicity on television requires the consumption of images, while an equivalent search on the World Wide Web necessitates the identification of relevant keywords. The English language provides numerous facilities with which I can define my ethnicity: ancestry, religion, cultural influences, nationality, countries of domicile, immigration status, biological traits or 'race'. Yet it is difficult to find words which move beyond where I come from and what I look like because our spoken and written language problematises ethnicity even though it is often heavily garnished with political correctness. When 'Pied de la Poulet' is listed in the menu of a posh Chinese restaurant, the poncy name may diminish the stark reality that it's chicken feet, but it will still turn the stomach of the most 'right-on' diner.

The dilemma of concentrating my identity into a few keywords manageable for a search engine is somewhat similar to substituting 'root vegetable fingers drizzled with coulis of tomato' with 'chips and ketchup'. Apart from the term 'Western Chinese', other keywords could have been:

- **Australian Chinese**: this implies a duality in my subjectivity and neglects the significance of having spent most of my adult life living outside of Australia, having a United States Social Security number and being allowed to vote in Britain. It suggests equal weighting between my Australianness and Chineseness when the latter is perhaps more visible and the former is kept at arm's length.
- **Black Oriental**: 'black' is not meant as a pseudo-scientific or biological category to describe a 'race' of people, but has been reconstituted by Afro-Caribbean and Asian communities in Britain to include all ethnic minorities who are subject to racism (Hall, Held and McGrew 1992).
- **people of colour**: part of a 1970s trend in the United States of referring to non-whites (Lippard 1992). Does this make me both 'black' and 'yellow'?
- **ethnic minority**: it has been suggested that this is a form of disempowerment through language as globally, Caucasians are distinctly in the minority (Lippard 1992).

- 'slopehead', 'chink', 'ching chong': re-appropriated and used ironically, with a perverse sense of humour, of course.

These alternative keywords are difficult to consume without feelings of discomfort and guilt. In an academic form of bulimia, they are constantly regurgitated and their contents inspected. Being rather sick of this whole process, I have elected to use what I perceive to be the most easily digestible of the keywords: Western Chinese.

The World Wide Web's offerings of Western Chineseness were both familiar and surprising, with a new set of courses presented with each search engine used. The buffet of choices included home pages of people of Chinese ancestry, artists combining Chinese and Western influences in their work, websites about alternative medicine, Chinese language print and broadcast media, Canadian Chinese fiction, cross cultural marriages and resources for studying Asian-American history.

The search engine, Yahoo, found two sites offering 'personal introductions and marriage services exclusively for Western men and Chinese women'. These were listed on the search results page, each with a brief introductory sentence – I did not visit the sites. This gives a whole new dimension to mail order, or rather e-mail order. I realise how limited my Littlewoods catalogue is: no section for potential spouses listed according to ethnicity. One of the sites was called Meow-Meow's Club which I guess is supposed to connote Asian tiger/Siamese cat-like Oriental mystique. Or it may be more analogous to stray cats on heat, unconcerned about pedigree and happy to cross breed.

Of course, my fascination with these e-mail order spouse sites is entirely academic: its representations of Chinese women as exotic Others work together with the explicit project of transcultural mixing. I wonder what falling in cyber-love would be like, what happens when matters of the heart and sins of the flesh are mediated by technology. Would I still have married my husband if I had met him this way? Possibly, if I could have erased from my mind the lingering suspicion that he might be a computer nerd. It is more likely that I would not have met him at all if the statistics about the Internet being populated by a 'white, middle-class bohemia' (Johnson 1996: 98) are true. His membership of white, working-class bohemia meant that other technologies mediated our relationship: the feats of aeronautical engineering brought him, 'two thirds English and one third Irish' from the home counties, and myself, a Chinese Australian from

Sydney, to New York City, where we met.

These cyborgian, syncretic intersections and interactions of Westernness and Chineseness are represented on the World Wide Web in ways which are rarely found in film or television. Excite found me an Etiquette Meeting Room (http://www.ibride.com/ibride/meetings/etiqroom/276.html) in which the topic of cross-cultural marriages was being discussed:

> [Message] 'I am Korean and my fiancé is Chinese. We are having a big western wedding, but I would also like to incorporate both Chinese and Korean traditions into our ceremony and reception. Anybody run into similar situations and/or may have ideas on how to do this?'
>
> [Follow-up message] 'I too am in the same type of situation. I'm Chinese and husband to be is Irish. We're going to have the invitation both in English and Chinese. We're going to have an American buffet, but all the announcement with *(sic)* be in both language.'

I was going to post a reply suggesting an internationally renowned wedding tradition – eloping – until I realised that the original message had been posted nearly a year ago and wondered whether that other popular marriage custom – divorce – was more likely by this time. In any case, it seemed almost blasphemous for a cyborg to advise on matters of tradition. I also felt a pang of regret that I did not have this electronic advice when I got married: I would have asked other hybrid couples what strategies they used to convince their friends that giving lots of cash instead of a gift was the usual practice at [insert whatever ethnicity as appropriate] weddings. I would have concocted any representation of my ethnicity as necessary to avoid our subsequent affliction with toast racks and tea cosies.

The rich array of pickings of Western Chineseness that I plucked from the World Wide Web contradict and complement each other, like finding fish and chips in many a Chinese takeaway. While many sites offer new ingredients to the old recipes of presenting Chineseness, others resort to stereotypical notions in making their claim of 'ethnic expertise'. The New Age Network China site, found by Yahoo, is 'introducing the western new age movement to China and chinese *(sic)* thoughts, religion, philosophy and qigong to the world'. Again, this was listed in the search results but not visited. It constructs an image of Chineseness which is complete and pure: anyone entering this dimension of Chineseness is subjected to a strict regime of tai chi and acupuncture; for any Chinese person, there is no escape unless s/he is knowledgeable about the healing properties of ginseng and the writings of Confucius. I would inevitably fail my entrance test to this world of Chineseness because as far as 'Chinese thoughts' are concerned, I can only contribute my own, which are in rather rudimentary Cantonese. Is there some consensus to what Chinese people think which someone forgot to tell me about? If contradicted, will bad luck fall upon my family and I in the best traditions of Chinese superstition? Perhaps there is much I can learn from the classic texts of the 'western new age movement' like *Spoil Yourself with Oil: The A-Z of Aromatherapy*; *Make a Living at Hair Braiding* and *Crystal Couture: Choosing the Right Crystal for your Aura and Outfit*.

The apparently mutually exclusive territories of Westernness and Chineseness are criticised by Said (1992) as European inventions. This 'orientalism', the construction of the Orient as the cultural contestant of Europe, is evident on the World Wide Web as well as television (such as in the character of Kelly in *Home and Away*), but is not entirely confined to Western perspectives. One site (http://www.cs.mu.oz.au/~lyk/exhibit/exhibit.html), found by Excite, advertising an exhibition by a Taiwan-born artist at the Australian Chinese Museum, describes her work as combining 'classical Chinese traditions with western use of color and light, to create a new way of depicting the classic Chinese subjects of landscape and flowers'. Logically, this means that prior to Western influences, the Chinese painted their landscapes and flowers in the dark, without any colour. I had no idea colour, light, geography and botany could have ethnic identities.

This 'Orientalist authority' (Said 1992) which purports to 'speak for' the Orient was also evident in an academic web journal, found by Lycos, which featured the topic of Chinese immigration in Australia and the history of the White Australia policy (http://www.ecuinfo.cowan.edu.au/ecuwis/docs/res/quest/mar96.html). An article titled 'Chinese in Australia: Challenging the Generalisations' was publicising the work of a Dr Jan Ryan, who has also written about the 'Chinese role in South Africa's transition to post-apartheid society'. My initial response to finding these web pages was to try to recall any Chinese person I knew with the surname Ryan. After all, I can rationalise my own narcissistic interest in Chinese presence in the West. The ethnicity of Dr Ryan remains a mystery, but what is baffling is why anyone who isn't Chinese would wish to examine my ethnicity for a living. Why Chineseness and not Black French Algerianness or any other arbitrarily chosen ethnicity? It is akin to my experience of ordering chow mein in a 'Chinese' restaurant in Romania where there was a total absence of Chinese employees, and eventually being served with spaghetti in a thick, soya sauce-flavoured gravy.

Such feelings of curiosity mixed with disappointment were also present when I read about Dr Ryan's research findings which revealed that the Chinese population in the state of Western Australia was not a homogenous group (gasp!!) but actually spoke different Chinese dialects (no!!). Those same feelings remained, sitting indigestible, when I saw another academic web offering 'Consuming the Other: Representations of Western Women in Chinese Women's Magazine Advertising' (http://orient4.orient.su.se/ chinese/perry/chicago.htm) by a Perry Johansson from Stockholm University. While the article argues that Chinese consumer culture is subject to an imperialising Western aesthetic in its images of women, its claims appear to be made from a position of Swedish, possibly male, Orientalist authority. These cultural intersections are both intriguing and disquieting in that knowledge about Chineseness is being broadcast across global networks to a seemingly small audience which seems to exclude the parties that are being discussed, who do not have access to this representational power and/or technology. Where are all the academic cyborgs (apart from in this book)?

This sort of Orientalist authority, claimed from outside a discourse of Chineseness, is difficult for a cyborg to negotiate without taking an essentialist position. After all, cyborg politics is about fluidity and hybridity, the antithesis of absolute binaries. Indeed, my intention is not to enforce boundaries of who lies inside and outside Chinese ethnicity. Rather, it is a plea for a declaration of position: if cyborgian activism seeks to reclaim the power to signify, then first we must know who is speaking and their relationship to who they are speaking for. What are their coalitions and affinities with those who they claim to represent? Are they acting for themselves or on behalf of others? If it is the latter, then the cyborg is obliged to interrupt, to 'insist on noise' (Haraway 1985: 95), and generally make a loud nuisance of herself. Where academic research is concerned, this might mean arguing for research funds to be redistributed towards marginalised groups rather than to those who assume an advocacy role. But this requires a statement of location, because without it, the world they observe is objectified.

This practice of making Chineseness an object of study and spectatorship is reflected and repeated in other broadcast media, namely film and television. A video on Chinese Canadians publicised on the web (found by Lycos at http://www.nfb.ca/FMT/E/MSN/17/17806.html) purports to give a 'first-hand account' of business and community life in Vancouver's Chinatown. Casting my eye over the production credits (presenter Fred Davis; director Allan Stark; producer Robert Anderson; photographer Donald Wilder; editors Marion Meadows and David Mayerovitch), I entertain the possibility that the production team are actually all Chinese but anglicised their names so as not to appear too biased in their representations of their own ethnicity. But I subsequently conclude that my imagination is talking bollocks. 'Western influence is apparent everywhere', the video's abstract proclaims, implying that there is an authenticity that is being eroded, as if the traditional recipes for sweet and sour, fortune cookies and prawn crackers will be lost forever.

A contrasting response to this perceived sense of cultural loss is given by the Asian Canadian community's website, Chinacity. The site contains short stories by a writer and playwright called Marty Chan (http://www.asian.ca/media/chinacity/confu.htm): 'Kung Pao Chicken. Eggrolls. Mu Shu Pork. Egg Foo Yung. Which China did this food come from?'

Chan's point illustrates the constant process of adaptation, integration, incorporation and mutation in Western Chinese cuisine, changing according to the supplies and demands of a particular locality. This dynamic state of Western Chineseness, this Fortune Cookie Phenomenon, not only applies to culinary matters but is central to the whole business of identity and cyborg politics. It's about new fusions, whether these be infusions or confusions, which may work elegantly or eccentrically or somewhere in between. Chan describes an example of such confusions: his parents' efforts to give their children a 'White' Christmas experience. He writes:

> Back in the Seventies, my parents hadn't a clue about the holiday season. They were fresh off the sleigh, but they tried to get into the spirit of the season. While our neighbours trimmed their trees, dad screwed together a Zeller's Everlast Tree Facsimile. Instead of tinsel and Christmas ornaments, he hung shredded Chinese newspapers and Oriental pin cushions ... Christmas dinner hit a little nearer to the mark. It wasn't turkey, but it was

close: Peking Duck ... Every year, I got money from 'Santa' in a Chinese red packet. Most years, it was twenty bucks. A few times, I got fifty. Once, I had an I.O.U..

Equating ethnicity with cooking and the combining of new and different ingredients to produce unusual and unprecedented flavours opens up the possibility of a Western Chinese ethnicity which does not necessarily speak, read or write the Chinese language. For example, while my World Wide Web searches under 'Western Chinese' produced many Chinese language sites, such as those of the Sing Tao Daily newspaper and KAZN, a Mandarin Chinese radio station in Los Angeles (both found by Yahoo), these are not representative of my ethnicity which is one of Cantonese-speaking illiteracy. Even using the numerous types of translation software that can be downloaded from the web to use in chat rooms, I would probably fare better reading and writing French or Spanish. As a cyborg, I can duck and dive from these affiliations.

Hybridised ethnicities produce surprises and contradictions, like when I once watched Ken Hom cooking pasta in his wok, and are represented in web texts such as those of Marty Chan (mentioned above) and Jason J Tobin (at http://www.momentum-hk.com/jason/intro.html), a young Eurasian actor, born in Hong Kong, who lives in Los Angeles, and was educated in Hong Kong, Britain, the Philippines and United States. These websites seem to assert our right to be mutants, to be Chinese and not Chinese, to be Western and not Western, to be continually undecided, and revel in the irony of doing so. This is reminiscent of an incident in my own life: when I had braces on my teeth as an adolescent, the orthodontist asked my parents whether they wanted my face to look more Western or more Asian. We agreed on a Western jaw structure and the orthodontist manipulated my teeth accordingly so that my physiology has since remained suspended between Chineseness and Westernness. While I have witnessed comparative transformations and fluxes of identity represented on the World Wide Web, in TV-land they seem more likely to appear in *The X-files* and pertain to extra-terrestrials than to ethnic minorities.

'The truth is out there' in cyberspace rather than in television's terrain. The recipes for ethnicity on television have been slow to change because of the lack of diversity of those doing the cooking. Those practices are also evident on the web, but collide with and diffuse amongst others which serve up dynamic and non-traditional images of ethnicity. Some of the untried combinations will invariably leave a strange taste in one's mouth, but are nonetheless an attempt at resisting essentialist representations of ethnicity through mixing, blending and experimenting. When online, one can at least sense the presence of cyborgs through their idiosyncratic political projects, whether these be marital, artistic, commercial, spiritual … and so on. Give me a buffet over a set menu any day.

Plugging into the mother country

Jules Cassidy
Sally Wyatt

Colonials or cyborgs?

THIS chapter focuses on plugs – one of the most mundane and taken-for-granted artefacts – which connect our domestic appliances to that huge technical system which emerged at the end of the nineteenth century. This chapter arose from a discussion between us while we were waiting for some of our colleagues to arrive at a meeting for all of the contributors to this book. We realised our recollections of arriving in England and being amazed at the absence of plugs on recently purchased domestic technologies were very similar. At the time, this peculiar absence was just one of many with which we had to cope. From the vantage point of our current awareness of the embeddedness of technology in social life, we understand how the plug has helped to police the boundaries between England and Empire, between England and its European neighbours, between 'real' and 'inadequate' feminists and between working and useless electrical appliances. Like Bruno Latour's (1992) account of door grooms, sleeping policemen and Berliner keys, this chapter illustrates how plugs play a role in ordering social relations.

Jules arrived in London in 1973, overland from Australia. Sally arrived in Brighton six years later, from Canada. We did not come as immigrants. Both of us intended to stay for a year or so, and then move on. We are both white, so our experience of colonialism is very different from that of our black Commonwealth sisters and brothers. But we both grew up in former colonies, with a strong feeling that the action was taking place elsewhere and that we lived in colonial backwaters, especially compared to the cosmopolitan ideal represented by London. In this chapter, we deliberately use the terms 'English' and 'England', not only because we live in England, but also because the colonial relationship is largely with the English, not the Scottish, Irish or Welsh, all of whom have their own unequal power relationships with the English and within the Union. Of course, we did not experience racism, but we did and still do endure disparagement and condescension about our home countries. Even the most politically correct English people often appear to feel no shame in making rude and offensive remarks about what they perceive to be characteristic of Canada, Canadians, Australia and Australians.

Despite our different origins, some of our early experiences are similar and they illustrate how even something as simple as a plug can play a role in maintaining colonial relationships, by making outsiders aware of their 'otherness'. In her story, Jules pursues this further and describes how, within this peculiarly English context of plugless electrical appliances, the ability to wire a plug becomes a test of one's feminist and lesbian credibility. Within English feminism, colonial power relationships are reproduced in the divisions between competent and incompetent lesbians. Sally also recalls her arrival in Brighton but then her recollections take her across the North Sea to the Netherlands in the 1990s. Her experiences there of different sorts of plugs, electrical appliances and other domestic technologies simultaneously made her feel both more and less 'other'.

This chapter thus highlights some of the problems with the cyborg metaphor because our experiences of plugs illustrate how even these mundane technologies can be used to create and maintain 'otherness'. We most certainly did not feel much pleasure in our encounters with plugless appliances or in the reactions of others to our perceived incompetence and subsequent anxiety. However, Jules's experience also illustrates how lesbian communities in the 1970s and 1980s attempted to build a more cyborgian identity precisely through the acquisition of technical skills.

Haraway's (1985) original cyborg thesis is imbued with a notion of 'outsider identities'. Pre-feminist lesbians lived their outsider otherness quite unobtrusively, moving in the shadow world of bars, or as the wives of men. In the 1970s, many of these women came roaring out of the closet pushing full tilt at boundaried constructions of gender. Reconstructing gender, building new identities, redefining the 'feminine' were integral to the lives led in the lesbian squatting communities. A woman with a hammer or an electric drill in her hand was powerful and political, a very potent cyborg. Yet even within this enlightened and radical place there lurked a malfeasant in the undergrowth that threatened to cast Jules into cyborgian oblivion, as her story recounts.

Implicit in our accounts are the advantages of being 'other', of the different possibilities for perception and action. Despite having to put up with the casual ignorant remarks made by many English people about our national heritages, we have both experienced real benefits as a result of our 'otherness'. Not being English keeps us safely outside their pernicious class system, granting us perhaps more social mobility, allowing us to assume partial identities with greater ease (Haraway 1985).

Sally's story: Both ends of the wire

Readers of my individual chapter elsewhere in this book will know that I grew up knowing quite a lot about power stations specifically and the generation of electricity more generally. When I was between two and five years old, we lived in Niagara Falls. As well as being taken to admire this eighth wonder in its 'natural' splendour, I remember being taken by my father to see the first turbines built to harness the power of the Falls, constructed sometime around the beginning of the twentieth century. I knew more than many children about the generation and distribution of electricity.

It was not until I came to England in 1979 that I realised how little I knew about electricity in the home. Growing up in Canada, I took electricity and electrical appliances for granted. You bought them, took them home, plugged them in and they would dutifully perform their designated tasks.

I arrived in Brighton in October 1979, to do a one-year economics course at the University of Sussex. I only planned to be here for a year, so had not brought many of my worldly goods with me. I lived in a shared house for postgraduate students on the Brighton–Hove boundary. The first shock was the two-bar electric fire that ate fifty-pence pieces and did not generate much heat. I have never felt so cold as I did inside that room during my first English winter. Sometimes I would put my nightgown over the fire to warm it before going to bed. More than one nightgown became singed.

Even though I intended to return to Canada after my course, I decided to buy a radio. I went to Woolworths and bought a simple radio, which I still have. It was in a box. I took it back to my room and took it out of its box. To my complete amazement, it had no plug. I thought there must be some mistake. Naive young Canadian that I was, I returned to the shop to ask for a radio with a plug on it. The staff treated me with the contempt the English reserve for colonials and told me I needed to buy a plug. To confuse me further, they asked me technical questions I couldn't answer: how many pins did I need, what amperage? How was I to know these things? I bought a plug and asked one of the English students to put it on my radio.

As one year became twenty, I bought more electrical appliances. I would occasionally try to wire a plug. Mostly, I relied on the goodwill of the people – women and men – that I lived with to do this tricky plug stuff. I use my colonial background to justify my technical inadequacy and consequent failure as a proper feminist. Plugs continue to terrify me. I am convinced I will wire them incorrectly, resulting in either my own death or major meltdown of the household electricity system. I no longer take electricity for granted.

In the summer of 1996, I bought a new stereo system. It took several hours and a couple of telephone calls to a competent lesbian friend, but I connected the CD player and tuner to the amplifier and I wired the speakers. All of the components came with plugs.

In 1997, I stayed in the flat of a friend in Maastricht while she was on holiday. Would electrical appliances and their plugs have the same power to make me feel foreign, as they had during my early days in England? I was much older and wiser than when I had arrived in England, almost twenty years earlier. I knew continental plugs were different from those eventually adopted as standard by the British; they were more similar to the plugs of my childhood.

I could not arrive in Maastricht until after Marieke had departed. I collected the keys from her secretary and made my way to the flat. Marieke had said she would leave notes on things, but I guess she didn't have time. There was only a brief note, wishing me well and exhorting me to eat her food and drink her wine (except for some special bottles on top of the wardrobe). The objects and I were on our own.

I walked around the flat and the garden. I found a couple of hangers and unpacked my suitcase. So far, I was familiar only with the doors and walls. I went to the toilet – first encounter with a foreign technological object. How to flush it? There was no handle, no chain, nothing to push or pull. But there was a pipe, from the cistern to the bowl, with the following words next to it:

spoelen
buis
omlaag
bewegen

WISA-KIWA

I know some Dutch, but these words were not familiar. The arrow was. I pushed the pipe down and achieved the desired outcome.

Flushed with success, I decided to check out the other technologies: telephones; stereo; TV and video; portable Toshiba; lights; very odd looking heaters which I hoped I wouldn't need; four ring gas hob; combination microwave and convection oven; washing machine. I tried the phones. In this small flat, there were three: late 1980s phone and answering machine, 1950s heavy black dial phone, 1990s cordless number. There were some red lights on the answering machine, indicating it was on but when I picked up the receiver there was no dialling tone. There was no dialling tone with the 1950s number. There was a tone with the cordless phone. Despite my difficult encounters with English plugs in recent years, I tried to figure out where the cordless phone was plugged in. I was rewarded for my efforts as I found the four-point plug that characterises Dutch telephones and, after some experimentation, I realised only one phone could work at a time. I wondered how Marieke decided which phone to use. I went with the one she had left in; thinking she must have had her reasons, even though this probably meant the answering machine wouldn't work. I'm not used to cordless phones, having never used one before. I believe one is supposed to be able to move away from the base unit. This seemed very magical to me. I had a few calls on my first night and I stood within inches of the base unit throughout them all.

I figured out the television and the stereo, but didn't bother with the video. These are global products, with international signs on them about what to push and when. I couldn't figure out the tuner/radio. It is the oldest piece in the system, and perhaps less global. I did manage to get music from the newer CD and cassette players. This is one of the benefits of the globalisation of production: as multinational corporations increasingly supply a global market with universal products, local differences disappear.

The plugs may be different but the televisions, stereos and dishwashers increasingly resemble one another. Seen one Sony CD player, seen them all. This can be very reassuring for a foreigner abroad.

Thinking I only had the shower left to master the following morning, I went to bed. I clambered over it in order to put on the bottom sheet, and discovered a black control panel. I pressed a button – the head of the bed tilted upwards; another button – down it went. Different buttons controlled the foot of the bed. More buttons controlled both simultaneously. I was speechless with wonder at this plugged-in bed. I had never been in such a high tech bed. It makes reading in bed much easier. I'm curious what it means for sex.

What are the stories behind these technologies? Where do they come from? Some – like the toilet – are clearly part of the flat. Others belong to Marieke. Did she choose them? Were they gifts? What lay behind the stereo which had been put together over many years? Why this peculiar collection of telephones? What is the story of the bed?

During the course of the week, I learned to operate the microwave feature of the combination oven. Over several phone calls, I developed the confidence to move further and further away from the telephone base unit. More technologies became visible – a transcription machine (Marieke uses ethnographic methods in her own research), a slide projector, an unconnected ancient fax machine, a less ancient but still unconnected printer, portable tape player, eleven lamps, no ceiling lights (except in the toilet), portable radio, juicer, mixer, toaster, espresso machine, a portable heater, three bicycles in the back garden and another two in the basement. There were also two old cameras, positioned on a mantelpiece as decorative objects. The significant absence from this list for an English person is an electric kettle, a technology in which Britain still rules the world. The juicer, the number of lamps, the absence of overhead light, the number of bicycles all suggest the Dutchness of the usual occupant.

While staying in Marieke's flat, I became used to the taste of fresh fruit juice. Juicers are much cheaper in the Netherlands, so I bought one to bring back to London with me. It has a two pin continental plug. I have not rewired it. I use an adapter. Refusing to learn to wire plugs is my minor act of resistance to the power of Empire and a reminder of my Canadian roots.

Jules' story: The plug and I

It wasn't until 1974 that I became conscious, in my adult life at least, of the unique and separate existence of the electric plug. Before that it was merely that fairly uninteresting bit at the end of the wire on an electrical appliance. Its most distinguishing characteristic was that it plugged into a socket which supplied the power to make the appliance go.

The plug often figured in Australian government posters and TV slots as part of a long running campaign to warn children about the dangers of electricity. These ads featured a cartoon character called Shocko. Shocko was an alluring, sardonic and rather fascinating character, drawn as a devil with horns and a cape. This shows that governments often get these campaigns wrong and end up making the forbidden or dangerous appealing to the very people they are meant to repel.

The air literally crackled around Shocko as he pursued his various adventures with wall socket, electricity and occasionally the plug. Sometimes he stuck his pitchfork in the socket, sometimes he stuck the plug in or pulled the plug out when the socket was on. Although these adventures invariably ended with Shocko getting spectacularly electrocuted, Australian children knew something the government did not: Shocko never got killed! Despite appearing with Shocko in these campaigns, none of his glamour ever rubbed off on the plug. Even the socket had more kudos, as Shocko often materialised through its holes. I, for one, was convinced that he lived in wall sockets and, of course, that is true.

Just before Christmas 1973, I arrived in the UK totally unaware that my personal relationship with the plug was going to change. In fact, I was about to have one. Backpacking through Asia, I bought a cassette player in Singapore. I had this fantasy of listening to Pink Floyd's *Atom Heart Mother* while watching the sunrise on the Himalayas. This did come true, although it might have been sunset. The cassette player needed a converter for its rather odd two-pronged plug in different countries on the hippie trail. When I got to London and moved in with some friends, I found that I had lost the converter and it was impossible, in those days, to live without music in my room. 'Don't worry' said my friend Joanie, a very practical university secretary from Melbourne, 'just cut off the old plug and put an English one on it'. 'I'm sorry, I beg your pardon' I replied. 'Yes' she said, 'there's millions of things like that. They're a bit odd, you know'. So it was that Joanie explained all about the totally strange phenomenon of English plugs. Like most Aussies in the UK, I was amazed that *you bought them separately* from the appliance. 'Why?' I asked Joanie. 'Maybe because they have all these different, strange sockets'. 'Why is that?' I inquired, but she didn't know.

With vague fears that Shocko might have moved to London, I set to work with a will because I needed that music. It was colder than I ever knew before, and grey. I missed India and I thought that Jimi Hendrix might help drown it all out. The problem was that I didn't really have the first clue about what I was doing. The plug had been a piece of black box technology up to that point in my life, a seamless, organic whole with the wire and appliance. Brown wire here, blue there, don't worry about the earth, it's only got two wires and what is that other thing on the right? It is important to know that I was the girl who got 28 marks out of 100 for sewing in the third form at Mordialloc High School. 'She holds a needle like a crowbar', wrote Miss Rometch, rather presciently, on my school report. Attaching a plug proved to be a very difficult task for someone as manually awkward as I can be.

I can't really recall the first appliance that I bought in this county, but I always felt that kettles, lamps and toasters looked undressed in some way with their bare wires trailing. Even big things like hi-fis, fridges and washing machines came naked; so undignified for them. The shops would always charge you extra for a plug, if they had any, but usually you had to buy it at a separate shop or from a market stall.

To us Aussies this was quite incredible. I had started to really feel my 'difference'. I was that stranger in a strange land. England was so odd with its impenetrable class system and weird shops like electric razor hospitals, newsagents that sold fags and sweets, eel and pie shops and whelk stalls. Every time I opened my mouth I became a stereotype. I was Bazza McKenzie. 'G'day Bruce,' the cabbies would say, mimicking the Monty Python show. The plug business somehow encapsulated it all for me.

When I first arrived in London I was, like many young Australians, on my OS (overseas) odyssey. I intended to stay in London for a year or so, explore Europe from my base in the mother country, and then move on to South America or the West Indies. I did not reckon upon encountering something that was almost non-existent in Melbourne but was thriving in London: the gay scene and the famous Gateways lesbian club in Chelsea in particular. This was a new world to explore that made Mexico or Brazil seem almost colourless in comparison. Life on the hippie trail was, after all, relentlessly heterosexual. After many adventures in the company of a group of similarly enthralled Aussie dykes, one intoxicating night in the Gateways, I fell in love with an Englishwoman and I was here to stay.

Folklore had it that, in the 1970s and 1980s, the London Borough of Hackney contained the highest concentration of lesbians in the world. Explanations of this phenomenon were much discussed and quite complex, but a neglected and eminently squattable local housing stock, the shortage of cheap, inner-urban rented accommodation and the presence of other lesbians were compelling reasons to locate there. I joined this community of women in 1976 and lived there, on and off, for six or seven years.

As Hackney's fame spread, lesbians came to stay from all over the UK, Europe, Australia, New Zealand and America. Many formed relationships, settled and became part of the community, while others stayed for a few weeks or months in the 'travelling women's house'. As relationships broke up, new ones started and children were born, there was much movement between houses and, with the constant influx of new women, considerable pressure for more houses.

Most of us lived in squatted Greater London Council (GLC) property that had lain empty and boarded up for many years. These houses required considerable work to maintain, but the fabric, plumbing and wiring were basically sound. However, as the community expanded, derelict Hackney Council houses (derries) were also reclaimed, wired, plumbed, and patched. Hackney dykes became notorious for their manual skills. Always a hotbed of different strands of feminism and radical lesbian thought and action, Hackney became central to the political movement around women and manual trades. Many Hackney women formalised their skills, becoming plumbers, carpenters, electricians or painters and decorators, running their own businesses, or working in the construction industry.

The senior tradeswomen in our midst were happy to share and pass on their skills. Thus when a new house was squatted there was always someone to help with the plumbing or electrics. However, as the houses needed constant attention, it became fundamental for all of us to be able to wield a hammer and use a screwdriver. As it was not really done to ask the trades goddesses in our midst to run you up some shelves for your bookcase or meditation area, even the most cack-handed acquired a measure of expertise that could be used or traded. To be a real Hackney dyke it was *sine qua non* to be able to do basic level DIY tasks.

Plumbing and electricity were always the most problematic areas. While elaborate strip washes in the kitchen were the norm for ablutions, bathrooms were gradually installed in the spare rooms of some houses. The weekly visit to the public baths for the extra soak before pool night was replaced by visits to 'communal bath' households. On Fridays and Saturdays, for obvious reasons, it was often necessary to book your bath informally. A lover in one of these houses was very handy as was a top plumbing girlfriend or mate who might just be persuaded to install a bath or shower at your house.

The houses were old and cold and the wind rattled through the doors, windows and roofs, in some cases. Of central heating there was none. Most of us were very busy with coming out of the closet and being radical lesbians, squatters, activists, writers, healers, tarot readers, mothers, pool and softball players, lovers, travellers, friends, students, cooks, gardeners and boulevardiers of Hackney. There was mega activity, but not too many jobs and incomes. Keeping warm, out of bed, was a major issue at wintertime in all households. Some of us developed intense relationships with our electricity meters, tending them lovingly, always alert for the visit from the meter reader.

Although I had lived in squats around Ladbroke Grove in west London for some time prior to living in Hackney, I had not picked up many of the necessary DIY skills. The thrill of the new squat wore thin fairly quickly for me. My English graphic designer girlfriend had very definite ideas and skills so I found it very easy to leave it to her. Hackney, without this lover, was a very different matter. I had been very ill with TB, depressed, and at a low ebb. Hackney was a new start. After a time I determined to get my own house with a friend: we decided to reclaim a derry. It was a doomed project for a number of reasons but it did kickstart some small competence in the DIY area.

Later I moved into another house with friends. My room was a small, snug, south facing back bedroom. It was previously occupied by a quiet, pleasant German woman who, unknown to all of us, had been a minor member of the Baader-Meinhoff terrorist group. She must have had rather strange ideas about colour, or perhaps she just wasn't bothered, because the room was a rather hideous brown and lavender. I painted white over most of the brown and stuck posters and pictures of various opera divas and footballers that I adored over the rest. The room didn't have a door and as doorhanging was definitely a skill beyond me, I obtained a large velvet curtain that did the job very well. The fireplace had been bricked in but the alcoves did very well for shelves and a wardrobe.

Knowing the Hackney etiquette, I constructed these very rickety edifices myself. This process was observed with some amusement and comment by my housemates, friends and lovers. Nevertheless, I felt I had done a fair enough job and my DIY standing was adequate. Sadly, humiliation was around the corner. Despite developing some DIY skills, my reputation was to be diminished.

How did this happen? In order to upgrade the appointments of my room I acquired a new tape machine and bedside light. It was therefore necessary to buy and attach my old nemesis, a plug, to both these appliances. The mistake I made was to try to do it in front of people. A few friends had come round for a drink and a smoke so I decided we needed the new light and sounds. Out with the screwdriver and some minutes later, I heard the dread words: 'Can't you even change a plug? Give it to me!'

I tried to explain about Aussies and plugs, how we had integral plugs with all appliances at home and that there was just no plug issue in Australia. I even counter-attacked with a bit of Aussie rubbishing of the 'poms and plugs' ilk but I knew I was doomed. My laid back butch image was about to go down the plughole. It would get out and go round that I couldn't change a plug. And it did. One night when I was being cool, drinking and playing some immaculate pool in the Queen Eleanor, someone laughed at me about it. Did it put me off my shot? As a notoriously thin-skinned Aussie, no doubt, though I won't swear to it.

Long before I came to live in Hackney I had got over the shock, my bemusement and the small amusement value of the English plug thing. I still regarded this technological system as perverse and irritating, but after it cost me my reputation as a true Hackney dyke it became and remains a matter of fear and loathing. Despite my understanding that self-reliance and independence from men was very much wrapped up with the acquisition of manual skills as both a political article of faith and a strategy for survival, I felt it was so unjust and unfair that competence with this particular piece of excluding technology should be a marker for credence in our community. Such strong feelings about a seemingly small and insignificant piece of technology.

Neither cyborg nor goddess

Of course the plug isn't an insignificant piece of technology. Today it connects the computer on which we wrote this to the electricity supply that powers its operation. The external modem through which Jules connects to the Internet sports an integrated plug on the end of one of its cables. Our laptops must be plugged into the mains for recharging. The plug is a simple but vital component of one of the 'old' technologies that has facilitated the so-called ICT revolution.

The advance of microwave, cellular phone, satellite and wireless technologies means that this may change but for the present the plug, dedicated or not, is an easily overlooked but important 'boundary' technology. The yin/yang embrace of the plug and the socket connects an array of business and consumer goods to the large technical system of the electricity grid. The socket contains all the power of a very large-scale technology; it houses the switch and is home to Shocko. The plug sits on the end of toasters, hairdryers, electric drills and lawnmowers, fax machines and photocopiers. The plug is domestic and mundane, curling up with pipe and slippers while it facilitates a night in front of the telly. The socket is so flexible that it can power a number of things at once – the sockets beneath our desks support Lego-type constructions of triple adapters and plug boards. Each one of these devices must, however, have its own plug if the nightmare scenario of constantly changing plugs from one device to another is to be avoided.

Jules remembers a hip phrase from the 1960s and 1970s: 'plugged in'. If you were cool you were 'plugged in'; you weren't 'socketed in'. Socket aficionados might try to claim to be 'switched on' but it doesn't wash. So plugs could be cool. The horrors and shame that we endured in our early life as young colonials abroad in England were really down to the whims of the socket. Standardisation, an important political and economic debate in many technological fields, brought relief to us both. Those diverse and demanding sockets were whipped into line. European regulations dictate that, like other sensible countries, the UK now has standardised sockets enabling dedicated plugs to be supplied on your latest juicer or video. This is immensely reassuring to us both.

For a time during twentieth century English life, the inability to wire a plug was a significant obstacle to achieving the status of either cyborg or goddess. Technological skill played a role in maintaining boundaries not only between masculinity and femininity, colonised and coloniser, but also between good and bad feminists. The hard-won technical competence of the Hackney dykes sometimes undermined the confidence of other women who struggled with technical tasks. For some English cyborgs, their abilities caused them to act superior to their colonial sisters, in much the same way that Englishmen do. It is for this reason that we suggest that the cyborg metaphor does not always have positive connotations: it can be used to divide women, precisely around the issue of technical competence.

The imposition of standards has rendered obsolete the skill required to wire a plug, so new tests of Englishness have to be found. Norman Tebbit, a prominent minister in Margaret Thatcher's cabinet throughout the 1980s, made the now infamous suggestion that one way of establishing immigrants' allegiance to the UK was to ask whether or not they supported the (usually losing) English cricket team, rather than a (more successful) team from one of the former colonies. Jules and Sally both fail this test: Jules because she supports Australia and Sally because she thinks it is the most boring game on the planet. And, in these allegedly 'post-feminist' times, who knows anymore what it means to be a proper feminist?

Growing up in the belly of the beast

Sally Wyatt

Introducing a cyborg family

WRITING this chapter has been a long process. The idea was first raised by Nod Miller at a departmental meeting in June 1996. I recall feeling both excited and apprehensive. What flashed through my mind were images of the family slide collection, which I had not seen for twenty years. On the rare occasions when the slides were shown, they would not be in any apparent order. Family groups were interspersed with power stations and other large engineering projects.

As a first step to exposing these visual and written images recalled from childhood and adolescence to my more remote adult gaze, I asked my father, the keeper of the slides, to send me a selection. My eldest brother collected them during a visit to my parents. My father sent some slides together with a short note which included the following sentence: 'Unfortunately, some years ago, because of the lack of appreciation of some of my slides, I threw out all the ones of the Melbourne rail yards (with the cricket ground in the background) and most of the power stations.'

My brother and I pored over these images from our childhoods in the dim light of a Chinese restaurant, trying to identify the artefacts and the people. My memory had not been entirely correct: not only were family holiday snaps mixed in with professional photos of power stations from around the world, sometimes the two worlds met. There is a picture of the Cornwall Hydro Electric Plant, taken during a family holiday in the Thousand Islands (where Lake Ontario meets the St Lawrence River) when I was four. There is another of me aged three standing proudly behind a Meccano crane bigger than I am, made by my 13-year-old brother. In my early childhood, we lived in Niagara Falls, where I was taken by my father, not only to see the water, but also the turbines which used the water to generate hydro-electricity. I grew up with technology, the real thing as well as visual representations and Meccano models. I would not have expressed it in these words, but I also grew up with the knowledge that technology is not only an important part of the social and political world but also of our symbolic universe.

My father was trained as a mechanical and marine engineer. He spent most of his professional life involved in the design and construction of nuclear power stations in Canada and elsewhere. He worked for Ontario Hydro, Atomic Energy of Canada and Montreal Engineering. I realised a long time ago that my father's life had been marred by the changing public perception of nuclear power. The sentence from his note, reproduced above, hints at his disappointment. When he started working on the thermodynamic cycles of the CANDU (CANada Deuterium Uranium) reactor in the late 1950s, the production of nuclear power for civil, peaceful use was the great hope of the future – a cheap, clean source of energy. In a letter to me (30 April 1999) he invoked imagery from Hollywood westerns to describe this:

The first major error by the nuclear industry was to think they had it made after President Eisenhower's famous 'Atoms for Peace' speech [1953 to United Nations General Assembly] which promised to make nuclear expertise developed in the nuclear weapons program available for peaceful purposes, particularly in medicine and nuclear power generation. Suddenly those of us, which included me, working on the Douglas Point design [one of the first operational nuclear power plants in Ontario, Canada, opened in September 1968 and closed in May 1984] became heroes in white hats and the weapons designers the baddies in black hats.

By the time he retired, he and his colleagues had become baddies in black hats, reviled by large sections of the public and also by their more immediate friends and family. He attributed this to a lack of public understanding and spent many years attempting to educate the public in his role as spokesman of the Public Affairs Committee for the Canadian Nuclear Association. As part of this mission, he wrote a book entitled *The*

Nuclear Challenge: Understanding the Debate. The book was published in 1978, a year before the Three Mile Island accident. He dedicates the book to 'the many thousands of people who have developed nuclear energy for the benefit of humanity'. I was given a copy for Christmas in 1978. I don't recall reading it. At that time, I was an undergraduate student at McGill University, discovering sex, substance ab/use and radical politics. When, in 1996, I decided that the time had come to read my father's book in order to write this chapter, I couldn't find my copy.

My mother is a writer of fictions and teacher of creative writing. She has always been a writer. She writes novels, short stories, radio and stage plays. I am proud of my mother: she leads an active and creative life, although, as many others close to writers have noticed, living with a writer is not always comfortable. In 1977, she published a novel called *The Rosedale Hoax.* It explores the petty concerns and snobbishness of one of Toronto's most exclusive neighbourhoods, where I lived with my parents during my last year of secondary school. The novel's protagonist, 'a gentle nuclear engineer, is burdened by an all-too-perfect wife, liberated children, an unpopular job, and the feeling that his neighbours are out to get him.' (cover). The book's dedication reads 'for Sally'. This I did read when it appeared. Scenes from family life can often be found in my mother's work which sometimes leave me feeling uneasy, as the experiences, conversations and feelings of others become 'material' and are re-worked into her fictions. A writer is always working. My feelings of uneasiness have receded over time, as I do more writing myself and know from my own experience that writers draw on many sources for their ideas. I also know that my versions of my childhood and family life are valid, even if not in print. As I become more tolerant in my advancing middle years, I even derive some pleasure from recognising people and events in her work.

These are my parents – Alan and Rachel Wyatt – and two of their texts. They emigrated to Canada from England, once in the 1950s and again in the early 1960s. I am the youngest of their four children, born in Canada in 1959. Between 1959 when I was born and 1979 when I moved to England, my parents moved house at least twelve times. My elder siblings moved even more. These frequent moves were because of my father's work: in the early years of my parents' married life, my father was in the British Navy; later, he followed the global techno-science of nuclear energy. My mother, brothers, sister and I followed him. My father's own experience certainly demonstrates that some knowledge and skills – like nuclear physics and nuclear engineering – are transferable, are not local. The disruptions we all experienced to our friendships and education, however, illustrate the local character of many social relationships.

In 1979, I went to England to do a master's degree in economics at the University of Sussex. I intended to stay for only a year but upon finishing my degree I was offered a one year job as a research assistant at the Science Policy Research Unit (SPRU). One year became twenty. My work at SPRU formalised my interest in technology policy and the social studies of technology, although I have never done any work on energy policy. In 1998, somewhat belatedly, I completed a doctoral dissertation entitled *Technology's Arrow, Developing Information Networks for Public Administration in Britain and the United States* (Wyatt 1998).

I see my family as a cyborg family: creatures and creators of reality and fictions who took holidays in the shadows of power stations; people who embraced their partial identities as migrants between countries and the 'two cultures'. C.P. Snow's *The Two Cultures* (1993/1959) was published the year I was born. The separation between arts and sciences that Snow condemned so vociferously was not to be found in my family. We incorporated technology into our lives in different ways; we made day trips to power stations and my mother even wrote it into her art. My parents had a variety of strategies for living with differences. I remember one funny occasion at a party for my mother's more 'arty' friends. My father, clearly tired of justifying what he did for a living, pretended to be the choreographer of a ballet company: a truly remarkable playing with identity for someone of my father's physical build. In addition to our frequent house moves and occasional country moves, we all moved between engineering and artistic worlds.

'Weaving is for oppositional cyborgs'

(Haraway 1985: 90)

In 'A manifesto for cyborgs', Haraway highlights the importance of writing, arguing that 'writing is pre-eminently the technology of cyborgs' (1985: 95) and that 'cyborg writing is about the power to survive ... on the basis of seizing the tools to mark the world that marked them as other. The tools are often stories, retold stories' (1985: 94). What follows is an interweaving of three retold stories: my father's *Nuclear Challenge* (NC), my mother's

Rosedale Hoax (RH) and my own *Technology's Arrow* (TA). This family dialogue of texts differs from Marianne's family history. Marianne is the neighbourhood poet in *The Rosedale Hoax*, who observes her neighbours from the safety of the family home:

> I have begun to write a family chronicle which will run to three volumes and be full of truth and the voices of my parents. This tape recorder is my notebook and soul and diary. This is not a multiple choice exam. All the questions must be answered. Mark the above statements out of ten for degrees of truthfulness. (RH: 16)

The extracts which follow will not always be assessed for their veracity but they do contain the voices of my parents. There is truth in all of them. I have chosen to draw from a text of mine, most of which was completed prior to re-reading the books of my parents. I selected and ordered the extracts but I have attempted to give us each a voice in order to minimise my unease with both autobiography and fiction in their treatment of 'others', who are always presented through someone else's perspective, sometimes as bit players and sometimes re-worked to fit narrative conventions.

I have also attempted to point to some of the connections. Most striking for me in re-reading these family texts are the points of similarity and convergence, especially between my father and I. Despite our disagreement about the particularities of nuclear power, I absorbed his awareness that the world is full of heterogeneous entities: people, animals, objects, nature, regulations, public inquiries. For me, reading actor-network theory later in life was not a challenge to my view of the world but a confirmation of what I had learnt in childhood.

Technology is social

In my father's reflection on the place of technology in society, he wrote:

> Our ancestors, out of the surpluses of their times, built houses, roads, railways, hospitals, factories, schools, mines, and harbours, which are now part of our resources. In the past, each generation has striven to bequeath to the succeeding generation more of these resources. Occasionally, the process has been slowed by natural disaster or war, but over the past 150 years, economic growth in the Western world has resulted in both higher

total and higher average wealth. (NC: 53)

[E]lectricity ... is like money ... In both cases, the barter process is cumbersome and inefficient ... In the energy case, electricity was developed largely because it is so convenient, easy to use, and versatile. With electricity, a person can keep warm, cook, create light, command a host of ways to communicate with others, travel, cut wood, drill metal, wash and iron clothes, and cut grass ... Even a seriously physically handicapped person can operate an electric switch. (NC: 29)

I share his perception about the importance of our common technological legacy:

Scholars in the humanities and social sciences have shown a widespread disregard for the place of technology in human affairs, yet artefacts and combinations of them play an important role in conditioning how individuals, organisations and political institutions conduct their daily activities. We live in a world inhabited not only by other people but occupied also by the material objects we and our ancestors have created. Sometimes we respond with awe and wonder at these feats of human ingenuity and creativity; more often we take them for granted and do not subject them to critical scrutiny. (TA: 7)

My father is keen to promote the benefits of technology such as wealth and freedom from drudgery:

If we accept that energy is one of the key elements of society then it is also axiomatic that energy is a political matter ... If one were seeking to destroy present society, a vital area to attack would be the supply of energy. It is interesting to speculate whether the reverse may not be true: are those who attack energy supply motivated mainly by the desire to attack present society? More frequently now there are attacks on nearly all aspects of technology, which has been made the scapegoat for all the ills of society. (NC: 16-17)

I am already convinced that technological knowledge is social through and through. Questions about how science and technology retain their cognitive and social hegemony and why the knowledge claims of science and technology are so rarely challenged will be left to others. (TA: 57–8)

Machine and electric energy extends that freedom [of choice] by freeing people, if they choose carefully, from much of the drudgery of life. (NC: 163)

The vicar, a character in *The Rosedale Hoax*, observes Bob Ferrand, his neighbour, the nuclear engineer:

Ferrand could have stayed on the peninsula growing peaches usefully. Instead of that he chose to go about littering the landscape with dangerous nuclear power stations on the pretext of giving the world light. Did he not know that it had been done already! (RH: 58)

Few of our political leaders are trained in science or engineering, yet the basic policy decisions in these complex areas are made by politicians. This is as much a criticism of the technical community as of the political world, since few technical people make the attempt to enter that world. Those who do ... find difficulty in adjusting to a world where talking about action appears to be a substitute for action. (NC: 158)

Technological development is dynamic. The modern Luddite is seeking to stifle scientific development for the benefit of humanity by imposing restrictions of scientific thought and experimentation unheard of since the days of the Spanish Inquisition. (NC: 161)

My father clearly recognises that technological decisions are also political ones, yet any questioning of technology is condemned as Luddite and his solution is for technically qualified people to enter the political arena, rather than to allow lay people to exert too much influence.

Engineers are human

My parents and I all recognise that scientists and engineers are people, products and shapers of their own time and place. My mother and father both address this theme, and they also pick up another with greater dramatic potential: the frustrations experienced by an engineer, sincere in his belief

LIVERPOOL JOHN MOORES UNIVERSITY
LEARNING SERVICES

about what is best but mystified and angered by the obtuse behaviour of, amongst others, politicians, environmentalists and his family. My father emphasises the benign intentions of his nuclear colleagues:

> Although we often talk of specialists and experts as though they were not human, they are people too. Like other people, they have families, they have religious and ethical convictions and they give careful thought to the future of the world in which we all live. The people in the nuclear business believe that nuclear power is the most environmentally benign way of meeting our present energy needs, and they have every sympathy for those who want to preserve and conserve our natural resources. (NC: 9)

Bob Ferrand returns home late after being with his mistress:

> Meanwhile the children slept. They were too old now to come looking for 'Daddy' in the night. He was in fact no longer 'Daddy', but 'Father' sometimes, 'You' often, and 'Him' in their private conversations. Sam might cry out, disturbed by nightmares in which his father, the villain, chased innocent people with balloons which turned into mushroom clouds. (RH: 7)

Sam, Bob's son who is at university, reflects on what his father does for a living:

> Sam thought that what his father did downtown was evil; evil as pyramid-selling, evil as piracy, evil as short-trading, as dealing in shoddy goods, watered wine, diluted drugs, and as throwing beer cans into clean lakes. Their argument was long since over. It had only become repetitive. Each could have taken the other's side like protagonists in a long-running play... Sam enters left, not smiling, and goes into his atmosphere-future-monster-children routine. Bob, not looking up from the newspaper, counters, with hysterical nonsense – read the figures – reasonably priced electricity – good employment – no accidents so far – what about coal miners. Sam speaks on behalf of windmills and solar energy. Taking out his folding easel and blackboard from his inside pocket, Bob draws a picture of windmills covering the surface of the province, the huge, striking flails far more ugly than any mill chimney or nice, round reactor building. Pulling his talking calculator

out of another pocket, he lets it speak, in its clipped Martian accent, of the costs of solar energy and the fact that still, with solar energy used in each house, the load on the local generating system would be excessive at peak times. The sun does not always shine, my son, and storage tanks are huge. Thus the arguments have become

> Repetitive
> Non-productive
> Except of hostility. (RH: 63-4)

Martha, Bob's wife, observes her husband:

> She could tell that at the moment his own work was depressing him. ... The delays in building, the constant hassle with the environmentalists, 'What do they think we are, monsters?', the fear that from now till retirement there would be no more worthwhile projects. All of it could make a man feel inadequate, impotent, and cause him to build an unreal, imaginary life and to make an enemy out of a harmless paper boy. (RH: 24)

Technologies are political

The difficulties of defining the scale and scope of technical systems and of where to draw the boundaries are addressed by all three of us. These definitional and boundary questions are important for understanding who should take responsibility for the 'side effects' of technical systems. My mother and father explore the roles played by politicians, political hearings and project managers in the development of complex technical systems, such as nuclear power stations. During the late 1970s, my father gave evidence to several public inquiries into nuclear power and participated in over 100 public debates.

My mother returns, in an ironic way, to the benefits of technology:

> At the Energy Hearing today, Mr. David Harvin proved conclusively that not only is nuclear energy extremely dangerous, it is also unnecessary. There was no reason why, he said, that the whole country should not be turned into a rural paradise. People, when they get used to it, actually like to have to fetch water from lakes, to go to bed at dusk and grow all their own needs with good, solid, iron-age implements. With this kind of living made compulsory, the need for power stations of any kind would gradually

disappear. The Committee has urged the government to suspend all further development of power plants so that the Harvin Plan may be fully investigated. (RH: 72)

Before leaving for a tour of the Middle East, the Energy Minister said that nothing was more certain than that, in the future, we must do everything we can to ensure the widest possible consideration of every known source of energy and that he will on his return from the tour, form three new committees especially for this purpose. (RH: 75)

In evaluating an engineering project, any competent professional engineer would prefer to use a systems approach. In simple terms, this means that the engineer would like to quantify, on a comparable basis, different ways of achieving the specified goal by considering all the aspects and effects of each option. Many energy and nuclear critics, when making presentations to non-technical and non-scientific audiences, will pontificate on the amazing new concept known as the **holistic** approach. In so far as it is any different from the normal systems approach, the difference appears to lie in including non-quantifiable value judgements of a social, moral, or ethical nature. If this is done, it has the inestimable advantage, to the critic, of making meaningless comparisons between different concepts, since the critic can conclude that the holistic approach proves the particular pet scheme of the moment to be superior to any alternative, without having to go to the bother of quantifying the case for it. (NC: 54, emphasis in original)

There may be widely shared notions of the distinction between 'large' and 'small' that are used in everyday discussion and in environmental groups' critiques of technology, but the distinction is not obvious in social scientific terms. If notions of scale are to be used in a descriptive, explanatory or prescriptive sense then greater precision is required ... [O]ne way of defining scale would be to rely on the perceptions of the actors ... Another approach would be to define scale in terms of the size of the dominant organisations involved in the operation, maintenance or regulation of the technology ... A third approach would be to focus on externalities – the scope of a technology's impacts on social and/or natural environments ... [W]hat are externalities but poorly defined impacts or impacts for which no one accepts responsibility? ... Another approach ... is to equate scale with riskiness, especially environmental risks ... Joerges (1988) argues that all of these approaches on their own are unsatisfactory. (TA: 66–7)

Bob Ferrand is interviewed by a journalist after the hearing:

"I'm not calling them corrupt. Only incompetent. They don't listen to the experts. They listen to the people who make most noise. Is that the way to run a country efficiently?"
"Efficiency is more important than democracy?"
"Surely you're not here to talk politics?" (RH: 99)

People have choices

In the condescending way of children, I was surprised to discover when in my thirties that my father was aware of the works of Jacques Ellul and Lewis Mumford. My father remains committed to the equation of technology with progress whereas I am more sympathetic to Ellul's and Mumford's concern about the spread of technical rationality. For me, techno-rationality is a powerful discourse which needs to be understood within a broader social context. Nonetheless, we are both critical of the ways in which these philosophers deny the possibility of human agency in technological societies.

Technological determinism often deploys images of 'big technology' – transport, power generation, communication, weapons. These are often what come to mind when we think of technology. Because of their size and complexity, both technically and organisationally, they can appear to be out of human control. But precisely because of the complexity of these big technical projects and systems, it is not surprising to learn that many people and groups with different interests will have been involved in their development. Yet, as these big technologies stabilise and acquire momentum, they give a very good impression of being autonomous and determining and beyond control. (TA: 19)

The dubious honour of founder of the anti-technology cult goes to Jacques Ellul (1954) ... Other leaders of this cult are Lewis Mumford (1967)... and Charles Reich (1971)...To these critics, 'technology' is imbued with an existence of its own which, in their view, is entirely negative and destructive.

Technology is accused of the following:

- Being beyond human control; from this premise it follows that its impact is antipathetic to people.
- Forcing people to needless consumption, thus 'technology' becomes the cause of human greed and the waste of Nature's resources.
- Forcing people to do repetitive boring work, which dehumanises them.
- Providing people with artificial diversions that destroy their chances for cultural self-fulfilment.
- Separating people from Nature, thus depriving us of our natural links with the world from which we came.

... The fundamental fallacy in all of them [above criticisms of technology] is the insulting assumption that we have lost our will to exercise any freedom of choice. (NC: 155-6)

[T]echnological determinism ... has two parts. Logically, the first part is that technological developments take place outside of society, independently of social, economic and political forces. New or improved products or ways of making them arise out of the activities of inventors, engineers and designers following an internal, technical logic that has nothing to do with social relationships. The more crucial second part is that technological change causes or determines social change. Misa (1988) and others suggest that what I have presented here as two parts of the whole of technological determinism are actually two different versions. Defining it as two different versions enables the scourges of technological determinism to cast their condemnatory net more widely by defining people like Winner and Ellul as technological determinists because they point to the inexorable logic of capitalist technological rationality. This is to confuse their materialism and realism with determinism. If they are to be accused of any sort of determinism, economic determinism is the more appropriate charge. (TA: 10)

The problem with technological determinism is that it leaves no space for human choice or intervention and, moreover, absolves us from responsibility for the technologies we make and use. This serves the interests of those responsible for developing new technologies, regardless of whether they are consumer products or *power stations*. Technological determinism allows all of us to deny responsibility for the technological choices we individually and collectively make and to ridicule those people who do challenge the pace and direction of technological change. (TA: 11, emphasis added. At the original time of writing, I didn't consciously include this highlighted example.)

Technology as cultural metaphor

Towards the end of *The Rosedale Hoax*, my mother uses the explosion of the atom metaphorically. Bob Ferrand has been caught out in his adultery and is moving to Calgary alone, without his wife and children. My father criticises this metaphor on the basis of what actually does happen during nuclear fission. I introduce another metaphor which captures our shared fascination with the real and figurative potential of technology.

They were sitting in this room disintegrating. A family, a group, unique in its relationship, with its particular memories and codes, was dying here. Fission was taking place: The atom when bombarded with neutrons, splits, but there is not necessarily a mushroom cloud. (RH: 105)

It is impossible for a nuclear reactor to explode like an atomic bomb. The design of a fission bomb requires bringing very pure fissile material together very quickly to achieve the explosive force. In a reactor, the fissile material is in very dispersed form, with large amounts of neutron absorbing and moderating material. This makes a bomb-type explosion impossible. (NC: 71)

'Technology's arrow' has two associations ... The first is with time's arrow, drawing our attention to the historical frame in which socio-technical events occur and the variety of factors which influence the trajectory of the arrow... The second association is with Cupid's arrow, capturing our fascination and desire not only with explanations of socio-technical change but also with and for technology itself. (TA: 155)

Fables for cyborg families

Nuclear power has considerable development potential for the future, which is the main reason thermal reactors are unlikely to become obsolete in this century. (NC: 119)

My father was wrong in this prediction. The accidents at Three Mile Island in 1979 and Chernobyl in 1986, together with growing public concern about safety, expense and waste disposal have meant that the nuclear power programmes of most industrialised countries have come to a halt. Maybe that is part of the reason why I have only now been able to relate my own interests in the relationship between technology and society to the writings of my parents over twenty years ago. I was then only dimly aware that my interest in technology was not simply one of intellectual curiosity: it was personal.

My parents and I write different sorts of cyborg stories, but they are all fables arising out of the socio-technical conditions of the latter part of the twentieth century. From our different but overlapping perspectives, we are each attempting to make sense of our worlds. We share a cyborgian sensibility of the relationship between the human and the technical and the impossibility and undesirability of attempting to separate them. My mother wrote stories to maintain her creative world, during decades when it was difficult for women to do so. My father wrote stories attempting to justify nuclear power. Unlike many engineers, he realised the technologies could not always be left to speak for themselves and that their muteness sometimes made them incomprehensible to other humans. He was one of their more articulate advocates, and his engagement with the technology is much more direct and normative than mine. As a dutiful youngest daughter, I too write stories about technology. Inhabiting a different world from either of my parents, I try to convince my social science colleagues to take technologies seriously.

Acknowledgements
I am very grateful to my friend Dave O'Reilly, a member of the techno-biographies group in its early days, who discussed the ideas and feelings raised during the preparation of this piece on many occasions. During the preparation of the final drafts, Hans Radder has engaged with me and this piece in substantial and meaningful ways. Most of all, I wish to acknowledge the love, work and support of my father and mother.

Section 2

Becoming technologists: on taking up (and making up) technological identities

HMTK meets HTML: from technofraud to cyberchick

Helen Kennedy

I am known to some of my friends as HMTK: Helen Mary Theresa Kennedy, recovering Catholic. This story is about my encounters with HTML (HyperText Markup Language, the scripting language of the World Wide Web) and other related technologies, throughout the development of my multimedia career. It is about my immersion into the world of new digital technologies and my journey from technofraud to cyberchick. The story is reconstructed from a diary I have been keeping for the purpose of technobiographical research for more than four years.

My journey from technofraud to cyberchick

I started my multimedia career in the Department of Innovation Studies at the University of East London in September 1996 as a researcher. I was employed initially on an action research project which explored the use of multimedia technologies in distance learning on a programme for mature women which was run in partnership with a local women's training centre. Although well-equipped for the job in many ways, I felt like a technofraud as early as the interview for the post. I remember taking a fearful inward gulp before answering a question about the Internet, something with which, at the time, I had had very little contact.

In post, my initial visit to the women's training centre provided me with the first of many encounters with non-stereotypical gender-technology relations: a group of rather untraditional geeks, women from a range of ethnic backgrounds, were employed there to teach various aspects of computing. The conversation about broken computers in which the women were engaged when I arrived provided a glimpse of their geekhood. After agreeing that an old computer should be disposed of, an Asian teacher asked if it really was broken, and a South American colleague of hers looked at me and whispered 'she wants to mend it. Sabina wants to mend everything'. However, this positive image of female technical know-how did not influence my constructions of my own relationship to technology in the diary I was keeping at the time, as the extract below demonstrates.

It's the second week of my new job in what looks like a technology department. My new workmate Mai and I go to the training centre round the corner for the second time and are greeted with the words 'is this the new uniform?' I am wearing tight-fitting grey pin-stripe trousers and a small black shirt. Mai wears baggy purple trousers and a black polo-neck top. Mai is Chinese and 5 foot 2; I am fair and 5 foot 7. We don't look the same. Mai and I laugh about it after. A friend thinks we must look like a pair of cyberchicks. Nice image, and Mai is a cyberchick: young, groovy, efficient, always doing something and at one with technology. I, on the other hand...

Today I faff around getting nowhere while Mai produces a questionnaire with great efficiency. I watch her out of the corner of my eye and learn all sorts about the mind of a cyberchick. The way that people send the mouse spinning around the screen used to bug me, but now I realise that they send it where their eyes are going. They don't read a page, make a decision about where to send the mouse and then send it there; they do all three at once. Mai reads a screen differently from the way I read a piece of paper: not starting at the top and working down to the bottom, but darting up and down and across and back and forward, not chronological at all. Cyberchicks read differently!

I am a technofraud. I'm full of doubts, fear and loathing. At home I am surrounded by the most backward technology in the land and at work I am the Woman of a Million Questions, when I dare show myself up. I ask Mai, I ask my neighbours, I ask the departmental technician and the IT helpdesk. Technology is getting me down.

I constructed myself as different to Mai in my diary because, at the time we started working on the research project, I felt that we were, technically speaking, extreme opposites. I felt daunted by her apparent knowledge. But I also enjoyed other people's perceptions of our similarities, for example when it was suggested that we were wearing a uniform. During the time that Mai and I worked together, a number of work colleagues and acquaintances confused our names despite our obvious physical (and other) differences. I played on this apparent confusion, introducing myself at work meetings immediately after Mai with the words 'I'm Helen Kennedy and I'm exactly the same as Mai', and suggesting to Mai that we should ring each other up before setting out for work and agree to wear the same things (we never did).

When I started my multimedia career, I had been using computers for a number of years, had used a range of software and had written about some aspects of domestic technology. I had a postgraduate qualification in cultural studies, out of which some cybertheory and other writing about new digital technologies has emerged. However, overwhelmed by the technical knowledge by which I was suddenly surrounded, intimidated by what I saw as Mai's cyberchick credentials, I felt my own lack of technical knowledge and competence very keenly and was afraid that I would be discovered and exposed as a technofraud. A year after starting work on the research project, despite these insecurities, Mai and I obtained a lectureship on a new multimedia studies undergraduate programme on a job-share basis; I am still the course tutor of that programme today. We shared a similar theoretical background and were deemed to have complementary skills for the job: Mai had practical knowledge of multimedia technologies and I had experience of innovative curriculum development and course delivery. Although the teaching of multimedia practice was not to be my area initially, my stark feelings of technofraudulence led me to undertake some courses in order to expand my knowledge of multimedia technologies.

So I embarked on a number of evening courses at a new media training centre to develop my knowledge of scripting languages and multimedia software applications. All courses lasted sixty hours over a ten or twelve week period. The first and last courses were advanced coding courses intended to develop existing knowledge: first Lingo and then HTML. The middle two courses were for beginners and focused primarily on software packages: first Adobe Photoshop and then Macromedia Dreamweaver (I now teach all of these topics myself). I chose these courses so that I could understand a bit more about what my students were learning in their practical classes. A different person taught each course. All teachers were relatively young (roughly between 30 and 45) and their dress code followed the alternative style of multimedia. In this context, my own dress – Camper shoes, Diesel trousers, scuffed, faux-leather red biker jacket, '100% polyamide micro' (like the fabric of anoraks) skirt with large, furry rear pocket – does not look out of place. (See Nod Miller's chapter in this collection for insight into a goddess wardrobe). In fact, it emerged that a T-shirt of mine, which has intriguing-yet-incomprehensible graphics on the front and back, was designed by a friend of one of my teachers. My own workplace wardrobe has shifted in a multimedia direction in recent years as I have gradually realised that it's acceptable for me to look how I want to, and to recycle my hair style and colour on a regular basis. I don't have to dress like a grown-up at work.

Of all the teachers on the courses I undertook, the biggest geek of all was the woman who taught my last course on HTML. She wore bottle-bottom glasses and undertook everything – her teaching, problem-solving and keyboard-operating – with confident precision. She had virtually no knowledge of software packages such as Macromedia Dreamweaver, designed to make web programmers' lives easier by making it possible to produce multimedia without knowing the code. With her impressive knowledge of HTML in its various manifestations and how to ensure its 100 per cent accuracy (not easy to achieve with a package like Dreamweaver), her life was already easy enough.

The other coding course I attended was about Lingo, the language behind Macromedia Director, the industry standard software for producing CD-roms. It is possible to make a CD-rom without knowing Lingo, but its interactivity is limited to click-here-and-go-there, or turn-sound-off-and-back-on-again. With Lingo, the potential for interactivity is much greater. The teacher of this course was an artist, yet his knowledge of the code was phenomenal. If multimedia = maths + art, then this teacher personified that equation. I wrote this about him in my diary at the time:

> The teacher is brilliant. He really knows Director inside out and appears to live and breathe Lingo. When we went out for a drink at the end of the last session, Michael, who I sit next to, said that he thinks that the teacher confuses Director with reality!

Clearly, I enjoyed studying these multimedia courses very much, partly because I felt that I was surrounded by people like myself: young folk with subcultural affiliations similar to mine always numbered amongst the teachers and fellow students. There were usually equal numbers of men and women, though I noticed gender differences on the Lingo course most of all. One female colleague clearly struggled and stopped attending after some weeks: her friend explained that she felt very disempowered by her Lingo experience. Another female colleague also stopped attending, and although she sent messages reassuring the teacher of her progress with her practical work, this never materialised. For the rest of the women, the course was a struggle. We shared our difficulties and frustrations and peered over each other's shoulders, trying desperately to learn from each other. In contrast, the progress of our male colleagues was less evident because, on the whole, they worked silently. One failed to come up with a final piece, but at least two others produced feats of complex programming during sleepless nights. In the end, however, we women eventually managed to produce a greater number of finished, functioning pieces of work than the men. For me, at least, this brought feelings of great triumph.

At the time of my third course about Macromedia Dreamweaver, I had been working in multimedia for more than two years and had developed my multimedia knowledge in a number of areas. By this time I had started teaching multimedia practice as well as theory. I wanted to learn about Dreamweaver in order to be able to teach students about it in the future and use it myself. I enrolled with two friends I had made on the previous course. My familiarity with multimedia, the place we were studying and some of the faces around me, along with the success of my practical projects on two other courses, meant that I embarked on this course with much more confidence than before. I was a relatively well-informed student to be participating in a beginners' programme, but I wanted the thorough knowledge that a sixty-hour course would give me. I certainly gained that knowledge and have continued to use Dreamweaver extensively, so in that sense the course was a success.

However, this course sticks in my mind because I had an unhappy relationship with the tutor. Towards the end of the course, we had a disagreement about the website project that I was working on, a real life website that was larger in size than stipulated in the course criteria. I mentioned this to the tutor before I began and he said that it would be possible to negotiate a bigger site if that fitted with what I was doing, so I set to work. On the day of submission, I thought it would be wise to remind the tutor that my site was large, which I had to do whilst he was at the opposite side of the room to me, as he declined to come over to me when I asked if I could talk to him – I was already not his favourite student. I reminded him of our prior conversation and he said quite simply that he couldn't remember it. I was amazed. He asked me how big the site was (admittedly, it was twice as big as stipulated) and when he heard, he said, in front of the other students, that it was selfish of me to make such a big site as it would take his time away from looking at other students' work, and he insisted that I cut the site up, removing most of it, even though this resulted in many links not working. For the rest of the session I cut my site up and couldn't participate in the activities of the class, much to my frustration, as my diary entry demonstrates:

> The teacher really enjoyed himself and I was a bit furious but mostly humiliated. Some of the other students tried to talk to me, but I couldn't speak to them because I was on the verge of tears. When I had finished, I left the teaching room, went into the toilet and burst into tears. I went back to the final session to get my mark, because I was concerned he would fail me.

However, I passed the assessment and received positive written, not verbal, comments from the tutor on the assessment sheet that he returned to me. I left that final session early for a prior engagement. In a later e-mail communication with a fellow student, she told me that when they had gone out for a drink that evening, one of the students had asked the tutor if he had enjoyed teaching us and he had replied that he found me difficult. I was really upset and didn't know what to do – confront the teacher, inform the training centre, or let it go? In the end, I did nothing.

Difficult encounters with multimedia men have also occasionally been a feature of my work in our university's multimedia production centre. The multimedia production centre, or MPC, forms part of the university's new purpose-built campus, which opened in September 1999. It houses the media and multimedia production facilities of a number of the university's departments. The MPC became my working home as a result of a visit to the construction site of the new campus. While a group of us who had been meeting to discuss the MPC's development walked around the site, it occurred to me that although several departments' production facilities would be coming together in the centre, no member of academic staff from my department would have an office there; instead, all would be housed in another building. I mentioned this to my head of department at the time, who was keen for me to consider locating there, so that our department was represented, and also to solve the problem of a shortage of staff offices elsewhere on the campus. Academic staff were, on the whole, being allocated offices on the grounds of whether they taught theory or practice: in deciding where to have my office, I felt, I was defining myself as *either* a theorist *or* a practitioner, but not both. As someone who teaches and does both theory and practice, I found this difficult. I was also torn between feeling that whilst practice is sometimes deemed cooler than theory, I found theory more peaceful. I also had to think about what it would be like to share a building with colleagues from a different department, who had previously been located on a campus six miles from my own, all but one of whom were men. I liked these people and felt that we had subcultural similarities: I had never been in a punk, ska or indie band as many of them had, but I grew up obsessed with similar music. I finally decided that having an office in the MPC would be a good move, even if it meant that I would be outnumbered by men.

The experience of being outnumbered by men has been common in meetings about the development of the MPC. The only exception to this has been in discussions about the development of a new multimedia masters programme based in the MPC, in which women have predominated and often provided effective leadership. Away from these discussions about 'softer' issues such as courses, our meetings about the development of the MPC itself – its cables, infrastructure and kit – have seen only a small number of women attend. I am the only woman who has attended consistently, and many of my diary entries about these meetings reflect on the fact that not only have I been the sole woman present, but also that sometimes it has been difficult to get my voice heard in such a context, despite my accumulating multimedia knowledge. Diary entries about these meetings such as the following are common:

> I was the only female there and no-one seemed particularly interested in what I had to say. I think I managed to get a word in once. I felt invisible.

According to my diary, one day last March I attended six meetings, all except one about multimedia in some form. The only meeting of the day that was not directly about multimedia was attended by a mix of men and women. Of the five multimedia meetings, there was another woman present at only one of them; together we numbered two women in a meeting of ten. The last meeting of the day was at 7 pm and took place in a pub. The time and place of this meeting wasn't unusual, as the predominance of young men in the field of multimedia means that going out and drinking is often a way of working and networking.

Another difficulty for me in the MPC is going to the toilet. I try not to let the number of men's and women's toilets there influence my feelings about the gender of multimedia, yet it does. There is one toilet with the symbol of a skirted figure on the door. There are three with figures in trousers, and behind one of these doors there are a number of urinals. I know this because on occasions when the woman's toilet, and I use the singular advisedly, has been out of order, I have used the men's. There are two toilets for people with disabilities, gender unspecified. Someone, at some stage in the development of our new building, made a revealing assumption about the numbers of men, women and people with disabilities of both sexes who are expected to occupy a multimedia production centre: of these three groups, able-bodied women were expected to be in the minority and able-bodied men in the majority.

Being outnumbered by men in multimedia (whether by male colleagues or men's toilets) is one thing; the way in which I have been outnumbered is quite another. I *have* found it difficult to get my voice heard, and I have very occasionally experienced difficulties with some male colleagues. Some of these colleagues appear unhappy with the changing working practices they have witnessed in recent years and dismayed at the unscientific ways in which much multimedia-related activity is approached today. Some of my interactions with these colleagues and their reactions to me have been upsetting. This may be because Mai and I appear to be visual icons of the changes they perceive to be happening, our cyberchick outfits contrasting starkly with the dress code of multimedia's laboratory origins, as one friend has suggested. Such encounters, however, have been in the minority. Mostly, I'm glad I chose to locate in the MPC because I have made great friends and have developed working alliances and allegiances with like-minded people. I describe myself and my MPC friends as young, even though I am

35 at the time of writing and the 'young people' in the MPC with whom I have enjoyed working are mostly older than me. It is typical of a university environment that such a group be seen as young, compared to the world of multimedia practice where, as one of the characters in Douglas Coupland's *Microserfs* comments, 'everyone over 35 is dead or maimed and out of sight and mind' (1996: 14). The predominance of such 'young' people in the MPC means that, in terms of age, it is older colleagues who are outnumbered.

My technofraud self of four years ago would have been surprised to see my cyberchick self involved in the production of a CD-rom card earlier this year. This was one of the MPC's commercial projects, which a team of MPC staff and students worked on collaboratively. The CD-rom we produced for the Knowledge Dock is the size and shape of a business card and functions as both. Once again, men outnumbered women in the team (the only other woman was a student who worked in a group to produce some video content for the card and with whom I had no direct contact) and once again we were all 'young'. The role of my male colleagues was to produce the assets for the CD: sound, video, 2D graphics and 3D animation. My role was to put these assets together and make them interactive using Director and Lingo. I did this during three and a half 16 hour days, a work pattern which would most suit people with no domestic responsibilities – say, for example, young men.

A freelance video practitioner who is sometimes involved in the MPC's commercial activities (though he didn't work on this project) was clearly impressed by my role as programmer. Every time we bumped into each other, he would ask me, wide-eyed, how the coding was going. At one stage, he was responsible for putting forward a report on the MPC's capability for potential commercial work, part of which was a skills audit. After I had listed my multimedia production skills to him, he asked me to spell out what, exactly, I had done on the CD-rom, about which he was obviously still intrigued. After I had done so, he concluded 'you could get any job you wanted with that!' His reactions to my multimedia practice, influenced as they may be by his own desire to become digital, suggest that my journey from technofraud to cyberchick, and the narrative I am constructing here, appear to be complete. Appearances, however, can be deceptive.

Gender, subculture and insecurity on my journey

In this story I have presented some of the events of the past four years, which I see as critical incidents in my journey from technofraud to cyberchick, through the usual processes of selecting, editing and interpreting-past-through-present-concerns that are common in writing autobiography. My initial aim was to tell a story about the cyborgian gender of multimedia – hardware, software, work and learning organisations. Clearly multimedia is central to my work experiences and identity, so I wanted to examine it, not so much in order to define it – its interchangeability with terms like digital media or cyberspace can make this a futile exercise – but rather to explore how it is lived. However, what started out as a gender story became something else, a story about the performance of multimedia identity more generally, as other themes emerged, notably age, subculture and the feelings of insecurity that exist in a multimedia context. I shouldn't have been surprised by the emergence of this cross-section of topics, as I am strongly influenced by Valerie Walkerdine's claim, quoted in the introduction to this book, that '[i]t is only the women's movement and the left which splits and fragments our history ... as though we did not live our class, our gender and our race simultaneously' (1989: 206). I also agree with Richard Johnson's suggestion that when we set out to tell one story, another, unintended story can sometimes emerge (Johnson 1997). In this section of the chapter, I reflect on these themes that surfaced in the previous section. First I explore what the events described here suggest about gender, but then I go on to argue that my story is about much more than gender, as the themes such as age and subculture also emerged. I finish by discussing the feelings of insecurity – mine and other people's – that appear in my account. In doing this, I problematise the apparently smooth transition from technofraud to cyberchick suggested in the chapter's title, and reflect on my use of such a binary opposition.

I wanted to write about the gender of multimedia because over the past four years, I've sometimes felt that it is masculine and at other times I've felt that it is feminine. In thinking in this way, I've drawn on the socially constructed binary opposition of characteristics that are usually attributed to men and women, even if these characteristics bear little association with the biological sexes. Although constructions of masculinity and femininity change across time and space and have proven themselves to be most unstable, assumptions about soft, caring and intuitive femininity and hard, rational masculinity are often still used in order to understand gender-technology relations. A central claim of Donna Haraway's 'A manifesto for cyborgs' (1985) is that such binary oppositions as masculinity and femininity have not been helpful in understanding techno-social relations: the construction of all technology as masculine, or of some technologies such as guns and computers as hard and masculine and other technologies such as microwaves and hairdryers as soft and feminine, is rejected in cyborg literature. The concept of the cyborg is proposed as a positive metaphor with which to understand complex relationships between humans, especially women, and technology. Initially, my aim in writing this chapter was to question, along cyborg lines, the idea that multimedia technologies are hard and masculine, or that cyberculture is a male-only space. Instead, I wanted to explore whether multimedia is neither masculine nor feminine but both, or whether, as Haraway suggests, such polarised terms are not helpful at all.

I wrote the first draft of my story with these issues in mind. In writing about the early days of my multimedia career, I wanted to draw attention to the existence of women 'inside' the world of multimedia computing and to reflect on what my construction of my relationship with Mai demonstrates about gender-technology relations. In order to draw attention to the constructed-ness of autobiography, I deliberately made my version of Mai quite controversial. The initial audience for the piece was Mai herself and other colleagues who worked with her, who might have questioned the accuracy and veracity of 'my' Mai. I wanted to contest the appropriateness of notions such as accuracy and veracity in autobiographical writing and demonstrate how, in autobiography, we interpret events and people in the past and present according to current concerns. My concern at the time was to understand my own relationship with computers by differentiating it from the relationships that I perceived others around me had with these technologies. In doing this I drew on those theories of identity construction which suggest that in order to have a sense of one's own identity, such 'others' need to be identified. For example, David Morley and Kevin Robins argue that identities are a question of differences in a system, that are 'constituted in and through their relations to one another' (Morley and Robins 1995: 45). In the diary extract, I constituted my identity in relation to Mai, defining myself as that which Mai was not. In writing

Mai as my other, I made sense of myself and my relationship to technology, positioning myself in opposition to Mai: she's a cyberchick and I'm a technofraud; she is efficient and I 'faff around getting nowhere'; she reads screens in a non-linear way; I read pages in a linear way; I ask, she answers. In retrospect, as I have already suggested, I feel I exaggerated my technical weaknesses in order to construct the women around me, including myself, as either technically competent or technically incompetent, a binary opposition. Such constructions suggest that I had access to a limited range of gender-technology discourses, so that acknowledging the complexity of women's relationships with computers along cyborg lines was not possible for me at that time. The limitations of my construction of our relationships with multimedia technologies as simply different were evident even at the time, as our similarities showed through.

I was also interested in gendered constructions of multimedia technologies themselves when I wrote the first draft of this chapter. In particular, I was struck by Karen Coyle's contribution to *Wired Women: Gender and new realities in cyberspace* (1996). She describes the association of computers with masculinity and male power, yet in her own references to the work of Steven Levy (1994) and John Dvorak (1995) this is clearly not the case for *all* computers. As both Levy and Dvorak indicate, the Apple Macintosh, or Mac, the predominant hardware platform of multimedia design, has been characterised as feminine in contrast to the masculinity of the PC. Levy writes:

> The previous paradigm of computing – command-based, batch-processed, barely coherent – was deeply associated in the MIS (Management Information System) community with masculinity ... Columnist John Dvorak contrasted the Mac with the new version of IBM's computer, the AT, and called the latter 'a man's computer designed by men for men'.
>
> (Levy 1994: 197)

According to Dvorak, the Graphical User Interface (GUI) of the Mac was 'girlish', compared to the 'masculine command line interface' of the PC (Dvorak 1995: 3, quoted Coyle 1996: 46). The masculine, textual, code-based interface of the PC and its application in computing was distinguished from the feminine, intuitive, graphics-based, multimedia Mac interface and its application in design; the implication, therefore, is that the non-textual, which includes multimedia, is feminine. This idea is expressed humorously by a female character in Coupland's *Microserfs*, when she describes why it is appropriate that she should work on the Mac format of a computer game whilst her male colleague works on the PC format:

> Windows is nonintuitive … counterintuitive, sometimes. But it's so MALE to just go buy a Windows PC system and waste a bunch of time learning bogus commands and reading a thousand dialog boxes every time you want to change a point size or whatever … MEN are just used to sitting there, taking orders, executing needless commands, and feeling like they get such a good deal because they save $200. WOMEN crave efficiency, *elegance* … the Mac lets them move within their digital universe exactly as they'd like, without cluttering up their human memory banks.
>
> (Coupland 1996: 120)

Masculinity lost the interface war, as the PC eventually incorporated a GUI, including many features that the Mac already utilised, such as metaphors: for example, the Mac has a trash can and the PC a recycle bin. Despite the fact that both Macs and PCs now commonly have GUIs, the association of the command line, or code, with masculinity and intuitive GUIs with femininity has not been forgotten.

Given these associations, it might be expected that the scripting and programming languages that lie behind multimedia applications are constructed as more masculine than graphical software packages such as Macromedia's Dreamweaver. Interestingly, this is not the case. The scripting languages that I studied, HTML and Lingo, both central to multimedia, are sometimes described as feminine, because they are not real programming. The reasons for this are different for each language. HTML is seen as easy and soft, even though it is as rational and logical as 'real' programming languages. The simplicity of HTML means that it is described as scripting, not programming. Although Lingo is very different from HTML, it is also sometimes described as 'not real programming'. Some programmers see Lingo as more chaotic and less rational than other programming languages. Perhaps the fact that it is a part of a multimedia software package means that Lingo is seen, by association, as not sufficiently masculine to be deemed proper programming. Its alleged femininity didn't stop my female colleagues and I struggling with Lingo on our course, however.

Like human identities, the ways in which multimedia languages like HTML and Lingo are viewed depends on what comparisons are made. Next to programming languages like C++, HTML and Lingo seem soft and feminine; compared to graphical software packages like Dreamweaver, Director and Photoshop, they seem harder and more masculine. Consequently, when I worked on the CD-rom card, my scripting work in Lingo seemed more masculine than the generation of graphical assets that occupied some of my male colleagues.

Multimedia environments sometimes seem masculine, either because men appear to feel more comfortable there (as on the Lingo course), or because they predominate (as in the MPC), or because, occasionally, they react in a hostile manner to the women they encounter in these settings (as on the Dreamweaver course). In the latter examples, I believe that gender played a role. I do not think that the Dreamweaver teacher or indeed some of my male colleagues in the MPC would have reacted to me the way that they have if I was not both young and a woman. Clearly many other factors were also at play, such as personal differences. So how do I know that gender was a factor? In asking myself this question I am reminded of a comment I made in my diary when writing about similar difficulties I encountered with two articulate, white, male students. I wrote:

> I think the reactions of these students have got everything to do with gender, though I haven't got any concrete proof of that.

The proof that gender matters is that, in my experience, it does. My suggestion that I was patronised or not acknowledged because I am a woman implies that at least some aspects of the gender binaries that the cyborg metaphor criticises remain intact. Despite my efforts to resist them, I find it impossible to reject these binaries, either because I feel that others operate them in their interactions with me, or because I mobilise them as an aid to understanding some of my multimedia experiences. Experimenting with cyborgian identities is difficult in such a context.

However, this gender analysis of my story provides only partial understanding of the events I have described here. What started out as a story about gender has become a story about much more, such as the subcultural identities of people who work in multimedia. The subcultural affiliations of multimedia people are evident in the diary extracts about my early multimedia career. I was trying to construct Mai and myself as opposites, but my attempts were not entirely successful. For example, our visit to the training centre clearly resulted in identification of our similarities. I acknowledge our sameness as well as our difference in that first diary extract and my comments, in which I point out that we were seen by some colleagues as not merely similar but the same. In the context of our work, similarities between Mai and myself were obviously perceived, despite my perception of the differences between us. As a result of this I engaged in two apparently contradictory acts, simultaneously constructing Mai and myself as different (in my diary) and the same (to colleagues). Similarities between us, as perceived by our colleagues and by Mai and myself, were subcultural. The clothes (and glasses!) we wore, the music we listened to, what we did in our spare time and the way we lived out lives, some of which were visible to our colleagues, meant that we were perceived as a pair of cyberchicks.

By using the term subcultural to describe the similarities amongst Mai, my MPC friends, the teachers and students at the new media training centre and myself, I want to draw attention to a number of factors which characterise these similarities: style, deviation from dominant culture and the relationship between the two, described by Dick Hebdige as 'the idea of style as a form of Refusal' (Hebdige 1979: 2). I've described the dress found in these circles not in order to marvel at our incredible sense of fashion but to indicate the subcultural style of multimedia. Similarly, amongst multimedia professionals, there is often (though not always) a history of resistant political activity, whether this be working on audio-visual projects with homeless young people, playing in a punk band or forming part of anarchic anti-capitalist movements – such activity is also central to my understanding of the term subculture.

I've described many of the multimedia people I have come across and made friends with as young, even though at 35, I am often the youngest. In my use of the term 'young', I imply an identification on the part of the people in question, myself included, with alternative subcultural lifestyles, characterised by the consumption and production of certain types of music and other media, ways of dressing and political affiliations. In such circles, previously pejorative terms such as 'geek' have been re-appropriated so that they are positive and complimentary: Ralph, one of the central characters of Neal Stephenson's cyberculture novel *Cryptonomicon* (2000), epitomises geek coolness. As subcultures are generally associated with young people, those of us who maintain subcultural affiliations as we accrue years could be described as performing youth in the same way that people perform gender. Thus youth can be seen as a set of practices which serve to include those of us who act out certain lifestyles regardless of actual age: just as masculinity and femininity are distinct from biological sex, so youth can, in this sense, be understood as distinct from biological age. Some colleagues who do not identify as young do not perform multimedia identity in the same way that my friends and I do. In a sense, they are the others in relation to whom we construct our youthful multimedia identities. Thus when older, harder IT approaches encounter newer, softer multimedia approaches, the interactions of the main actors are informed by an interplay of subculture, age *and* gender.

My story is also about the feelings of intimidation that both men and women experience in the face of multimedia computer technologies. My own early lack of confidence with computers is clearly stated, yet the insecurities and fears of others in relation to new technologies are also present in my story, albeit in less explicit ways. In *Knowledge Dock: new landscapes* (the CD-rom card whose production I described above), the director of the Knowledge Dock claims that technology today is developing at such a phenomenal rate that technical knowledge is quickly redundant. He states that 'the exponential rate at which technology is developing over time means that the usefulness of information that is relevant to any particular job is decaying at an ever-increasing rate'(Multimedia Production Centre 2000). Although claims like this are questionable and not new, the prevalence of such ideas can lead to insecurity about whether what we know still has value and, if it does, how long its value will endure. In such an environment feelings of insecurity about our knowledge and our futures are difficult to resist, even for me, where my apparent knowledge could be seen as new, which, according to the hype, is more valuable than old knowledge. The freelance video practitioner's construction of my technical skill could also be seen as another example of the insecurity that pervades these technologies. His responses to my work and knowledge could be understood in terms of his own feelings of disempowerment in the face of new media, as he tries to update his own analogue skills. In ICTs, the constant proclamation of the death of the old leads to feelings of career instability for some, who may then project total employability onto someone like me, regardless of the fact that I don't experience this for myself.

Not such a straightforward journey after all

Learning about multimedia – hardware, software, scripting languages, people, organisations and theorisations – has been an empowering experience for me. I enjoy both the creativity and the geeky problem-solving that working in this field allows. However, despite this sense of empowerment, my own feelings of insecurity, which were evident at the outset of the story, remain. I have presented my story as a journey from technofraud to cyberchick, in order to give it both narrative structure and narrative closure: the metaphor of the journey is common in autobiography, fiction and other types of writing. Such a structure inevitably hides the ups and downs and, in my case, insecurities that continue long after the narrative is closed. In contrast to the story presented here, I was still describing myself as a technofraud in my diary eighteen months after starting my multimedia career. The more I knew, the more I realised I didn't know. It was only two years after starting the job that I began to acknowledge my multimedia knowledge, after having contributed to the development of multimedia undergraduate and postgraduate programmes and the MPC, attended multimedia seminars, conferences and courses, developed a network of multimedia contacts and made a handful of websites and CD-roms. Even now, with even more of the above and some publications on the subject (for example Kennedy, Leung and Miller 2000 and Kennedy 1999), I don't really feel like the cyberchick I am perceived to be by others and have presented myself as here. The fast pace of change in this industry and the myth of the even faster redundancy of related knowledge form part of my experiences and, along with historical insecurities in the face of computing technologies, mean that my feelings of technofraudulence have not left me completely.

The technofraud could be seen as the binary opposite of the cyberchick: the former suggests exclusion from technology, whereas the latter implies a gendered resolution of techno-identity and declares my status as multimedia insider. The story I have told here suggests that I have made some progress from one side of the binary to the other but, for me, there is no final identity resolution after all. The construction of my multimedia identity will be continuous, with tensions and contradictory feelings an integral part of the project.

So what started out as an attempt to write a cyborg tale about the flexible and unstable gender of multimedia has turned into a story about the interplay of gender, subculture and insecurity in a multimedia context. I've found the cyborg metaphor useful as a tool for understanding the range of relationships that women have with technology, as it allows me to acknowledge the variety of ways that women engage with technologies, many of which are characterised by technical competence, skills and knowledge. In my story it is clearly not the case that men and women relate to multimedia technologies in gender-stereotypical ways. For example, the freelance video practitioner appears to lack the confidence that Mai, in contrast, exhibits.

However, despite my attempts to interpret my experiences through a cyborg lens, some more stereotypical explanations of gender-technology relations remain convincing. Other binary oppositions – technofraud and cyberchick, old and new – have also been useful in my story. Overall, my account suggests that the binary oppositions that are rejected in the cyborg literature are not so easily rejected in practice. Furthermore, although I embrace technologies, as Haraway suggests we should, the ways in which multimedia technologies are constructed result in feelings of fear and insecurity which are difficult to overcome completely, despite my accumulating multimedia knowledge. My story suggests that I am not alone in this. The incidents I have described here also indicate that application of the cyborg metaphor needs to extend beyond the usual focus on gender. My exploration of the ways in which multimedia identity is both lived and performed indicates the importance of taking into account the subcultural tendencies of the people who populate multimedia environments. As one of my former students recently said of multimedia, 'it's a bit punk rock'.

Acknowledgements
Thanks to Roisin Battel for providing me with a beginning to this chapter, by pointing out the similarity between my initials and World Wide Web code, and to Trevor Webb for providing an ending in the form of the above quote. Thanks to my co-editors and to Maciek Hrybowicz, Linda Leung, Andy Minnion and Sally Wyatt for comments on later drafts of this chapter. Special thanks to Andy, whose copious and colourful comments were poems unto themselves.

Technology and romance in the laboratory: reflections on being a 'normal' woman scientist

Gwyneth Hughes

I spent a large part of the day rushing up and down stairs collecting glassware … The other researchers seem friendly and fun but they don't notice the smell … Today has been promising. I intend to work slowly and carefully and keep calm in any crisis.

This diary entry from 1979 narrates my thoughts as I installed myself at a discoloured and scarred wooden bench with my assorted collection of glass apparatus. I was in a chemistry laboratory about to begin a year of 'real' post-graduate research at the equivalent of masters level. Throughout this period I kept a diary that reflected on both the technical and social concerns of a novice researcher. It was not written to document the experience, nor would I have ever imagined that extracts would be reproduced for public consumption; indeed I am unsure why I wrote it. The oscillations between elation and frustration or near despair, written in unreflexive, laboratory notebook style, initially surprised and shocked me as I read it for the first time twenty years on. The daily entries seem to provide a catharsis for a very troubled mind; after all I had only just emerged from the instability of those torturous teenage years. Alternatively, it could be read as an account of a woman's temporary respite from, but ultimate submission to, the alienation of science and technology. Yet I read this diary today as more than this, as an attempt to make sense of crossing boundaries in a puzzling world of contradictions concerning science, technology, gender and sexuality, combined with the unpredictability that was laboratory life.

In the extract above I seem simultaneously determined and apprehensive, but to understand why this should be so, some background might be helpful.

How being normal has its contradictions

Although I left school as a qualified female scientist, an apparently successful product of single-sex education and second-wave feminism, by the time I wrote the entry I had become a very reluctant chemist, finding my undergraduate experiences of laboratory work an endurance to be dispensed with as quickly as possible. Despite left-wing leanings and a sense of social inequality and injustice gained from reading writers such as Orwell at school, I had become seduced by the prospects of high-class living.

Throughout these undergraduate years, I desperately wanted to belong, to have a large circle of friends, to have a social life. Although I came from a white, middle class and educationally privileged grammar school background, I had never come across the wealth, the confidence and the capacity for partying that the majority of my contemporaries at this elite university possessed. They buzzed and hummed with excitement, gossip and intellectually stimulating ideas. I wanted to be a part of this too, although I did not admit to this desire for upward mobility at the time. My friends studied humanities and social sciences and many were involved in university politics, theatre or media with apparently little use for science and technology. Like them I believed chemists to be shy, dull and uninspiring and best avoided. I therefore played down my identity as a scientist whilst, at the same time, allowing my status as a woman scientist to give me certain intellectual credence. I glowed with pride when other women were impressed by my success in a male world. Nevertheless, before long, any enthusiasm I had for being a chemist had evaporated, fuelled by a succession of impersonal and uninspiring lectures and ignited by several frustrating technical incidents in the laboratory. Love of my chosen subject turned to loathing. No longer the pioneer for women's equality in science, I felt myself to be an outsider, a misfit, a maverick, yet I did not wish to give up completely this seemingly hard-won status.

So I inhabited two seemingly disparate worlds: the socially aspirant and the scientific. I desperately wanted to be a success in both. Social life meant an abundance of heterosexuality and, although I lacked the glamour, wealth and sophistication of many of my contemporaries, a three to one ratio of males to females at the university stacked the odds in my favour. However, despite a succession of 'boyfriends' and plenty of social engagements, I never felt a sense of belonging. I hovered on the periphery and was at my most comfortable in small groups of close female friends with similar backgrounds to my own.

But the following story is not just about the struggles of a woman scientist to become accepted as normal, of a woman dissuaded by the 'masculine image of science' (Kelly 1987) or of post-adolescent obsessions with sexuality and social life. It is about the complex intertwining of science, technology and human lives and the resultant paradoxes that I can now, with hindsight, analyse. As I wrote this diary entry, there seemed to be a chance to marry the two divergent cultures in blissful hetero-union. I could be part of a team of scientists in a triumph for feminism, deal with anxiety and dislike of laboratory technological work, meet some new men and improve on my social life too. Yet, as I shall go on to explain, here also was the germination of the idea that science and technology are socially located as well as an appreciation of the limiting regulatory norms of a compulsory heterosexuality that I would later reject.

Technically in love? A laboratory romance

But back to the beginning of my story: I had spotted an interesting looking male PhD student working in the laboratory, Mark.

> I have made a serious error and will have to repeat my reaction. But Mark was friendly, he asked me to play squash and helped me run my NMR spectrum.

The other researchers were, like me, aiming for academic qualifications. Four of us were first year postgraduate researchers, while the remaining four or five were established PhD students. We all worked for Dr N, as he was affectionately yet respectfully named. Dr N visited us daily, cracking jokes to lighten the atmosphere while supervising and directing individuals. Although we were doing his work (his name appeared first on the paper that was eventually published), each student had his or her own piece of pure science to pursue and I was quite unaware of this hierarchy of ownership of knowledge. Despite the absence of any collaboration, PhD students were clearly expected to give technical help to the novices.

The NMR (Nuclear Magnetic Resonance) was, from what I recall, a large sophisticated machine with small holes into which we inserted samples for testing. A printout of the spectrum emerged, as if by magic, after the pressing of a few buttons. Mark's help in my use of the machine had a double function here – initiating me into the rites of passage in the use of laboratory technology and clearly signalling the potential for a relationship. He was the most handsome male working in the laboratory – tall, dark and silent – and he had given me special attention. With this excitement to keep me thinking positively, the shame of making stupid mistakes did not dampen my enthusiasm for research for long.

All laboratory instruments were housed in separate rooms. After this user-friendly encounter, the NMR machine became my favourite. Perhaps this was also because it was the largest, most mysterious and most modern of all the laboratory technologies. I would insert a thin glass tube containing my precious sample into the machine, follow a straightforward sequence of operations and wait for a paper trace to emerge like the giant slow motion pulse of an electro-cardiograph. Later, while I was sitting at my bench, Dr N would lean over my shoulder and jab a finger at small perturbations in the graph making pronouncements as to whether this was indeed the signature of the compound I was seeking. My heart racing with excitement, I watched with fascination as he squeezed his tongue out through a gap between his two front teeth, deep in thought. However, sometimes he would shake his head at evidence of impurities or errors as I would compliantly agree to relive the lengthy, tedious laboratory synthesis.

> I enjoyed the laboratory work. I have crystals possibly ... compounds that haven't been prepared before ... Then Mark made me lunch in his room – tinned spaghetti – but it's the thought that counts.

Chemical synthesis and preparation of lunch appear to be essentially similar activities, yet they were associated with such different meanings. The laboratory work involved the preparation of organic compounds by adapting well-established recipes. I learnt quickly that synthesis of a previously unknown substance was the main aim of my research, provided that I could demonstrate this originality satisfactorily using the range of accepted laboratory technologies, including the highly esteemed NMR. As I was rewarded with praise from my peers for making a new compound, I gained the confidence to initiate a date with Mark. Whilst he stirred his coffee nonchalantly with a contaminated laboratory spatula, I hinted to him about lunch (something along the lines of finding a cleaner, more pleasant environment to eat in). I was rewarded for this boldness with an invitation to his room in college. Mark's unadventurous method of food preparation – heating up a tin – seemed very far removed from the creativity and originality we aspired to at work. But I expected no more from him, not just because I knew male students hated cooking, but because I was a social success now and this was far more important than my need for appetising food. Lunchtime invitations were followed by dinner dates and a romance began.

Mark had a large room in a newly-built postgraduate wing of a wealthy and prestigious male college with surprisingly good, and probably greatly under-used, cooking facilities. It was much more pleasant than my cold, damp and shared rented accommodation, with wiring so old fashioned that we could not even run a small electric fire. However, it was his sound system, at the time called a 'stereo', that impressed me most. I watched entranced as the layers of dots on the turntable transformed effortlessly to vertical lines as the album revolved. The speakers produced a clarity of sound I had not heard before; every small intake of breath from the singer was audible. Mesmerised by this glimpse of Mark's luxurious lifestyle, I immediately wanted a quality hi-fi sound system too. When Mark informed me that he was about to sell the speakers and replace them with larger, more powerful ones, I told him of my desire.

A few days later, drawing on my hard-earned summer vacation money and the remainder of my grant, I bought his speakers from him, along with a turntable and amplifier of his recommendation. Back in my dingy flat, he assembled and tested the system for me. Since I had little idea how to connect the components, I was relieved and pleased at this offer of help. On reflection, I am struck by the different rules for appropriate gender behaviour that applied inside and outside the laboratory. Whereas in the laboratory, Mark, as the more senior researcher, was expected to instruct me in the proper use of technical instruments, in the context of my flat and our emerging relationship, there were no such expectations. I was happy to watch him exercise his technical skill and felt no need for explanations or for guidance for future use.

With music and chemistry in common, I was convinced that Mark and I would get along very well. For a while, I basked in the pleasure and status afforded me by my acquisition of material possessions and my successful performance of heterosexual femininity. Yet my position was precarious. The diary entries oscillate between elation and dissatisfaction. Some days I enjoyed my work in scientific research, other days were clouded by anxiety and despair. Social interactions were invariably significant throughout these peaks and troughs.

> A frightening day in the labs because we had safety films and lectures which put me off doing any more chemistry ... Susan made remarks about me having lunch with Mark – I wonder how much they've guessed.

Susan was a PhD student who worked on a bench adjacent to mine. She was my idea of a stereotypically dull and conventional female scientist and I therefore tried hard to differentiate myself from her. She was a Christian, a Thatcher supporter and had a steady partner; I was an atheist, a socialist and my relationships with men rarely lasted longer than two weeks. She was an 'outsider' in that she had studied for her first degree at another university; I had achieved some sort of acceptance here from my undergraduate years. She wore large frame glasses; I wore contact lenses. However, despite our differences, Susan became a supportive friend for the remainder of the year. I boasted to her about my newly acquired heterosexual status and took pleasure in being the centre of coffee room gossip and speculation.

One morning, a jet of water shot out of my inadequately constructed apparatus and drenched a portion of the laboratory. This drew everyone's attention and laughter and I felt my absolute incompetence to be exposed. It was Susan who pointed out that technical disasters happened to everyone and she who helped me appreciate humour in the incident. I soon noticed that other accidents occurred and their perpetrators also became the butt of teasing and joking. For example, when another novice researcher, Kevin, spilled one of his samples onto the floor, filling the room with a smell more offensive than rotten eggs or cabbage, we threw open the windows, pulled faces and teased him for the remainder of that day. His notoriety as a noxious sulphur chemist was firmly established from then on. He appeared to relish the reputation but I doubted it would do him any favours in attracting friends or partners, and could not empathise with him at all. In addition, whilst I joined in the frivolities, I began to feel more and more uneasy about some of the risks we were taking; the stern warnings of the safety films preoccupied me but I kept my thoughts to myself.

No sign of Mark in labs this morning. He eventually appeared at 12.30 saying he'd been in agony with a stomach pain and hadn't been able to move till then. I believed him.

As well as the attraction of Mark's materially advantaged lifestyle, I admired his credentials as a scientist. He was a meticulous worker who never seemed to make mistakes, although he may just have kept quiet about these. I believed him to be a brilliant chemist. He would assist me in assembling apparatus with painstaking care and I became dependent on his presence in the laboratory for scientific as well as social status. Yet I became increasingly frustrated by the lack of sparkle in this relationship. My initial curiosity about my silent and mysterious mate was wearing off as Mark's reticence and now ill-health dominated. Now that our mutual interest in sound systems had been exhausted, conversation dried up. There was no passion, the relationship was clearly going nowhere and yet I still relied on his presence in the laboratory and felt abandoned and lost in his absence. When the inevitable break-up occurred, I outwardly agreed this was for the best whilst privately feeling sad, disappointed and confused.

I am still maintaining an interest in my work but of course I don't feel quite the same about the laboratory. I don't know why I feel like this since I know we're not suited.

I was embarrassed that the other researchers clearly knew that my laboratory romance had ended, and found their tacit acknowledgements of this unnerving. I accepted that the emotionally sterile relationship could not continue, yet felt resentment too. The romance that had provided me with an effortless entry ticket to the scientists' world and had made me a 'normal' woman had now gone. Could I achieve this acceptability through my work alone? This, it seemed, could never be a smooth journey and the following days were filled by a succession of technical hitches, accidents and errors as I continually chastised myself for my stupidity and carelessness. It seemed that the social and the technical worlds were never very far apart as I began to view myself more and more as an outsider to the scientific, as well as the social, world.

I had a long lunch break with Brenda (my flatmate). My crystals melted over lunch in the sun. I was teased of course. Susan quite rightly told me off and it meant a whole day wasted.

I was dismayed to find that an over-extended break had cost me a morning's work and Susan, who had quietly and tactfully replaced Mark as my mentor, delivered one of her many lectures on the need for constant vigilance and reliability. Her other favourite topics in these outbursts of moralising included stealing from the laboratory and promiscuity. Gender was very significant in both cases. The former was directed at the male chemists who purloined chemicals to add spice to student parties. They would arrive armed with dry ice to sneak into drinks so that a glass of wine would hiss furiously and boil over, much to the horror of the unsuspecting and perplexed non-scientists. I enjoyed this particular trick, as it confirmed my identity as one of the enlightened scientific fraternity who understood how it worked. I was less convinced about another prank of spiking drinks with pure, laboratory-distilled alcohol. I had drawn a boundary between harmless fun and thoughtless irresponsibility. For female students, Susan pronounced promiscuity as the most serious offence and, after my short relationship with Mark and my confessions of past liaisons, I felt sure she included me in this category. However, she did not need to use morality lectures to embarrass or reproach me into conscientiousness. Much of my work regulation and discipline was self-imposed.

Despite finding only sporadic enjoyment in the laboratory, I now threw myself wholeheartedly into my work, determined not to let the failed romance dull my endeavour to be a successful scientist. I resigned myself to the boredom of routine laboratory work distracting myself with juvenile workplace banter concerning Kevin and his noxious odours and the latest student crushes on Dr N.

The work was very repetitive: assembling glassware, heating mixtures, employing trial and error and attempting to isolate any products. However, the monotony was interspersed with occasional high points. I enjoyed the suspense of watching liquid revolving in a flask in the rotary evaporator (a piece of laboratory apparatus for removing unwanted solvents using a rotating glass flask). Usually, after a long, anxious wait spent gazing across into the laboratory opposite looking for distraction, the flask would empty, leaving me with hollow frustration. But occasionally I would be rewarded by the sight of crystals settling like snowflakes around the sides of the spinning flask. A gamble had paid off and I now had a product to analyse. These moments of elation contrasted with the more common and interminably routine ones and while I was excited by the prospect of breaking new ground, I felt distant from laboratory life and frequently longed for the year to end.

One day I noticed that Caroline, another first year researcher, was wearing make-up and smart clothes. Her bright red lips smiled at me excitedly across the room. She probably wore similar attire on other occasions but I distinguished this particular instance because Mark was spending a considerable amount of time helping her. They would disappear for long breaks together and soon became the centre of gossip. I suppressed a feeling of inner turmoil, of despair and jealousy that she appeared to be succeeding where I had failed, by trying to view her position with critical detachment. I thought her foolish to dress up for such dirty work. My old jeans, like everyone else's, were stained and full of holes. Swayed by Susan's puritanical disapproval of the relationship, I began to feel superior to Caroline because it soon became apparent that she was falling behind with her research, despite Mark's valiant attempts to keep her going. My determination to complete my thesis grew despite my increasing alienation from the work environment. Incongruously, even when my work looked promising, I thrived on my hatred of the laboratory, a martyr to a cause I no longer truly believed in.

Towards the end of the term, Dr N talked to all the first year students about our future plans. We knew he was canvassing for us to stay on as PhD students. After complimenting me on my success so far, he asked me whether I, too, had considered future options. A wry smile told me of his expectation that my answer would be a refusal. I told him I was considering enrolling for a Post-Graduate Certificate in Education and he nodded supportively. If I had shown any interest, I am certain he would have encouraged me to continue research – there was no overt discrimination against women here – but we had a tacit understanding that I was not cut out for such a career. Yet I had little appreciation of what research beyond this level might actually entail. I did not view myself as situated at the bottom of a hierarchy where novices perform the tedious ground work in exchange for experience and aspiration to a higher and more creative level. My understanding of the role of higher education was twofold: to gain qualifications and to make friends. Unlike some of my more ambitious contemporaries, who were busy carving out places for themselves in politics, media, business or law, I did not appreciate that I too might have access to a prestigious career. I could never imagine myself in Dr N's, or even Mark's, position. I could only conceptualise more of the same disheartening laboratory routine.

After the Christmas vacation with my family, away from the University, I returned to a chilly New Year.

I awoke to six inches of snow and had a dangerous and slippery cycle (ride) into the labs. Things are interesting in the laboratory, Mark and Caroline seem to have had a big split-up and are not speaking. Susan was intrigued.

Six inches of snow must be an exaggeration, drawing on popular imperial measurements and the poetic licence of the everyday world rather than the metric precision expected of a scientist. Nevertheless, I do remember being horrified to find a layer of ice on the inside of my window that morning. The laboratory was cold and deserted apart from Susan and Kevin, the most dedicated researchers, and a faint, sour yet sickly odour permeated the air. But soon others returned and the room warmed up with speculation on what had happened to the happy couple.

Now that Caroline's romance had also ended, she, Susan and I began to spend more time together both in, and outside, the research environment. Since I had decided that I would stay for only the minimum one year period, my diary for the remainder of the year makes fewer and fewer references to my laboratory experiences, detailing the importance of social life, especially female friendships, and plans for my next career move. I spent more time with groups of friends from my undergraduate days and some new friends, as well as with my co-workers. Relationships, built up between co-researchers, continued outside the laboratory and when Mark invited me to a party, this compensated for a dreary day. Despite my ever-decreasing confidence, the fantasy of the laboratory romance and of becoming a normal scientist remained with me, albeit in a diluted form.

Another expensive (on glassware) and frustrating day. Susan gave me a lecture on being too hasty.

As students, we were required to put down an equipment deposit which would be returnable at the end of the year after deductions for breakages. Susan continually joked about the unlikelihood of my having any deposit left to collect given my accident record. I laughed with her but I saw my growing breakage total as symbolising my unsuitability for the job and Susan's lectures simply served to reinforce this. I can now see that the late nights and resulting poor concentration and tiredness, common place in laboratory work, were probably the cause of many of my technical problems and accidents, but at the time I blamed myself.

Despite my increasing alienation from laboratory work, my self-imposed imperative to finish 'my work' continued. I was aided by Dr N's quiet presence, overseeing every stage of my work to ensure that I was producing useful material. Waiting for supervision with Dr N took up considerable amounts of time. I would sit at my bench, bored and listless, half-heartedly pretending to be working while he was locked in deep discussion with one of the PhD students. I am sure that I was not alone here. We all vied for his attention, resenting anyone who held him in conversation for too long, thereby depriving the remaining students of valuable consultation time. Eventually, I would attract his attention. I never considered continuing under my own initiative; he sanctioned every experiment I embarked upon. These supervision sessions were exciting and stimulating, especially when he told me that my work was original and opened up new possibilities for the synthesis of a set of new substances. Thus, I had many opportunities to re-cross the border back into the world of science. But I was easily dissuaded.

For example, one synthetic route Dr N pointed me towards filled me with fear, and although I did not admit my weakness to him, I confided in Mark and canvassed others for advice.

I found my next reaction involves cyanide and I am petrified of doing this and was too cowardly to have a go after reading the poisons book. All the others said it would be fine in the fume cupboard.

Such reassurances enabled me to complete the task successfully and my fears proved ungrounded. In fact, the most dangerous experience I ever encountered lay elsewhere and could not have been anticipated. Whilst working in the spectrometer room, adjacent to the main laboratory, I noticed that one of the solvents had an unfamiliar and unpleasant odour. I opened the window for fresh air and continued working for a short while but eventually left the room in disgust. I did not realise the danger until a day later when I overheard a conversation from another group of researchers who also used the spectrometer room. Apparently, the solvent had deteriorated in sunlight and produced phosgene, a deadly nerve gas, and when I told them of my experience they replied that it was fortunate that I had not remained in an enclosed space with this for too long. I was horrified at this totally unexpected apparent brush with death. Yet a few years later, belonging to a different scientific community as a chemistry teacher, I retold this tale with embellishment and relish, as one of heroism, of the pursuit of science in the face of danger, to groups of suitably impressed A-level students. It is difficult to assess the seriousness of the original incident after so much reconstruction, but at the time it seemed worrying enough to vindicate my decision to escape the laboratory.

I still don't feel I ought to spend the rest of life doing chemistry although Dr N said my work was going rather well.

I was delighted with the quantity of original and acceptable work that I had for my thesis which I laboriously produced on a manual typewriter. Had I been too hasty in rejecting a research career? I was amazed at the unpredictability of chemistry. Sometimes days of meticulous, concentrated work would produce nothing, whereas a synthesis thrown together carelessly at the end of a frustrating day could yield surprisingly fruitful results. It seemed unfair that there was no guaranteed reward for hard work and adherence to the correct rules and procedures. Since I did not believe myself to be capable of good research, I assumed my success to be more attributable to luck than expertise. I did not recognise that my experience and judgement might well be significant in these apparently random, lucky breakthroughs. A dualistic framework of thought meant I could be either a talented researcher or unsuitable for the job; negotiating the space in between did not appear to be an option then. So, with these thoughts in mind, I had only minimal ambivalence about packing up and leaving at the end of the year to begin my teaching career.

A cyborg story?

How has Haraway's cyborg metaphor informed my re-reading of my diary and my telling of this story? There are three themes that I would like to draw out and discuss more explicitly. Firstly, in this autobiographical story, I take an anti-essentialist view of identity concerning gender, sexuality, class and being a scientist. The account demonstrates that identity positions with respect to science and technology are not opposing and mutually exclusive alternatives to be 'chosen' or 'forced' into. Like Haraway's cyborg identities, they are contingent and shifting, constantly relocated and reinterpreted in time, space and culture.

Haraway explains that: 'The cyborg is a kind of disassembled and reassembled, post-modern collective and personal self. This is the self feminists must code' (1985: 82). Through this exploration of the construction of my identity, I have exposed a series of contradictions that arose from my class and gender positions with respect to science. I was in an elitist institution, yet was not one of the elite and, although I aspired to material wealth, I had little desire to enter the corridors of power. I felt incompetent with laboratory technologies and continually frustrated, yet I took pleasure in new and sophisticated technologies such as NMR spectroscopy and a state-of-the-art sound system, and I delighted in technical success and impressing friends with chemical know-how in our party tricks. I depended on a heterosexual romance and the respectability this gave me, as well as the support of a mentor, yet I had little desire to form intimate or long-term relationships with men and sought refuge in female friendships.

I have explored relations of gender, class and sexuality in my story to show that a science laboratory was not a comfortable space for a young, unsophisticated woman. However, my story is not a simple tale of exclusion. At any moment in this collection of minor, random incidents, I could have determined that the tedium and unpleasantness of research is rewarded by belonging to a lively community, or I could have taken pleasure in technological and intellectual achievement, and entered a PhD programme. The laboratory romance could have blossomed into a long-term affair with all the social and material advantages such conformity to heterosexual norms might bring.

Yet, despite the oscillations of my diary entries, there does appear to be an overall shift in my perceived position from belonging to 'unbelonging' in normal science. Given these contradictions, it seems hardly surprising that this was not a straightforward transition; there are lots of stops and starts, hesitations, possibilities for back-tracking and reversals. Through my laboratory romance, a closer understanding of, and respect for, masculine values seduced me into taking pleasure in the beauty, status and power of technology, whether hi-fi equipment or the technologies of chemical synthesis and analysis. I could appreciate the humour of technical disasters and relish the risks, enjoy initiating non-scientist friends, and later pupils, into an unknown world of unexpected mystery and danger. Yet such pleasures were fragile and easily disturbed. The failure of the romance brought with it a loss of belonging and security and made me less tolerant of the routine, the frustrations, the risks and the less engaging aspects of chemistry. My emerging criticisms of science made sense only through a rejection of the research life. Similarly, there are signs here of a recognition that a heavy investment in heterosexuality to achieve social acceptability is not the only possibility and that female friendships have value too. However, my subsequent taking up of a lesbian identity and my aspirations to belong in a very different world is another story not presented here.

I am cautious about pushing the cyborg metaphor to its limits. The reassembling of my post-modern self produces an almost linear narrative, a sense of wholeness rather than an arbitrary collection of fragments. This has been a deliberate choice on my part, both to give my story an overall theme about not being a 'normal' scientist and to provide insight into the exclusivity of the scientific world.

In my second use of the cyborg metaphor I follow Haraway's position more closely when I expose contradictions in discourses of science and technology as rational, predictable and separate from the human world. Thomas Kuhn (1962) applied the term 'normal science' to fact-gathering or puzzle-solving activities in science that occur within existing paradigms. Haraway further explains that all knowledge is 'situated' and dependent on the social and cultural means of its production. In my story, I describe how this supposedly normal scientific activity is unsystematic, unpredictable and open to interpretation, although at the time I clearly thought it was my methodology that was problematic.

The contradictions I describe demonstrate how science is as much a product of fluctuating social and cultural values as is any other activity in life. A successful scientist was supposed to be rigorous and meticulous, yet I found breaking the rules to be very fruitful. I produced work acceptable to the scientific world yet my means of production were unorthodox and I considered myself unsuitable for a future career in science. The laboratory was a place of humour, gossip, sexual relations and co-operative human activity yet at the same time a place of danger, unpleasantness, tedium, competition and isolation. My work belonged to me for the purposes of an academic qualification, but I had little control over its production or dissemination. My work was directed by my supervisor and owned by him for presentation in the public domain.

A rejection of objectivity in knowledge production leads to the third cyborg theme of this piece. By refusing to separate 'actual events' from their reconstructed telling, this story challenges the truth/fiction binary. In the use of the diary extracts there is no attempt to present the whole, and the use of de-contextualised fragments is a deliberate ploy to show that these are springboards for reflection rather than 'evidence' for the truth of the account. I make it clear that the diary is probably exaggerated when I question the accuracy of the six inches of snow and confess to embellishment in the retelling of the 'brush with death' incident to question the 'truth' of the event.

Haraway is not afraid of 'partial perspectives' (1991: 183) and celebrates the existence of multiple accounts. I am clearly retelling this story from my current position as an academic in Science and Technology Studies, as a feminist and as a lesbian. If I had a different position and a different politics, I might be telling a different story. About 15 years ago, I wrote an essay using this same experience as evidence of the discouragement and exclusion of women from science and technology to maintain the 'masculinity' and status of science. I still recognise that, even after the initial excitement and enthusiasm for research, I abandoned attempts to become a 'normal' scientist. Yet I do not now interpret this as a story about overt exclusion from, or discrimination against, women in science. Nor is it solely about being compelled to fit into normalising class, gender and heterosexual cultures, whether inside the laboratory or outside. I see it now as a story about a woman negotiating invisible contradictions and attempting to find some congruity in the face of only partially recognised inconsistencies, about treading a cyborgian path in almost complete oblivion. This is not to say that my earlier interpretation was wrong or unhelpful. A more straightforward account of women's exclusion from science could be much more useful for taking a strong political stance than a cyborg story could ever be. However, I now feel that a cyborgian account illustrates the inevitable partiality of all autobiography and avoids the dangers of claiming to tell the 'truth'. In this sometimes painful, if illuminating, probe into my past, I see that there are an infinite number of possibilities, an unimaginable number of other small incidents that, for various reasons, I have left out of my tale.

The past lives of a cyborg: encountering 'space invaders' from the 1980s to the 1990s

Linda Leung

THERE are many statistics that have illustrated the under-representation of women in technology-related higher education and occupations. According to the National Council on Educational Technology in 1996, women constituted only 17 per cent of students of Computer Science and 22 per cent of the IT profession. These figures differed from the findings of the Department of Trade and Industry which stated that as little as 13 per cent of students of computer science were female, while an even lower percentage entered the IT industry (*DP Connect* 1997). This construction of technology as a male domain has been compounded by popular images of 'hackers' as nerdy, young, socially inept men, and 'cyberpunks' as North American men between 15 and 30 years of age (Squires 1996: 200).

The following episodes provide some insight into my struggles as part of the gender and ethnic minority within these percentages and illustrate my insistence that I am not, by default, a female whose technical incompetence is compensated by fabulous social skills. They offer a qualification of the quantifications, exploring the gaps and cracks at the macro level through a microscopic examination of a couple of critical incidents in my life. The first short story is set in my childhood, the second in my adulthood, not only spanning time but also public and private realms. Nevertheless, the stories highlight technology as a tool with which I have contested and negotiated the boundary between inside and outside, asserted my Otherness and located myself in a place where I am not meant to be, thus staking a claim to a position of relative power.

The 1980s

Somewhere in his youth or childhood, he must have done something good. Or so my brother must have thought: to be born male, into a Chinese family and to be rewarded so handsomely for it at Christmases and on his birthdays. For example, in 1981, he received an Atari Home Entertainment Console which, at its retail price at the time, must have required my parents to take out a second mortgage. In today's terms, it would require them to rob a bank. I told my then 10-year-old self and my younger sibling that, as a matter of policy, any presents we received were really for both of us, and that he would be welcome to use my newly acquired wind-up jewellery box at any time. I learnt early that technology was a valuable currency for transgressing gender (and other) dichotomies. If I could broker a sharing arrangement, then it gave me licence to play in 'boy' territory and perhaps my parents would be less inclined to regard toys in such gendered terms. If sharing wasn't an option, then I would lay my claim to it anyway, operating covertly to use the gadget when my brother wasn't present and inviting my girlfriends around to do likewise. I was secretly delighted that not only could I probably match him in a video game challenge, but I also looked better in the trinkets from my wind-up jewellery box.

I subscribed to that policy until 1983 when I received a Speak 'n' Spell (ironically, the 'and' was spelt without an 'a' or a 'd'), an educational toy which succeeded in teaching me to spell 'colour' without a 'u' and 'judgement' with only one 'e'. At this point, it seemed that the policy needed to be updated to account for all the rights and responsibilities of the relevant parties, so I rewrote it along the lines of 'touch anything that belongs to me and you're dead'. I quietly justified this about-turn as affirmative action and therefore part of a major political struggle. After all, being Other was a licence to be contradictory, wasn't it? As it turned out, my brother was not remotely interested in learning to spell words without vital letters in them. He was too engrossed in riding his new Yamaha PeeWee mini motorbike in anti-clockwise circles around the backyard. If it became monotonous, he would change direction and if he got bored with that, he would return to his Atari console which, eventually, he found tedious as well.

This was understandable considering that the underlying principle of Atari games was 'blobs', not the technical term, but the most appropriate because all the graphic objects in the games did not resemble anything other than blobs. The developers must have thought that children would never tire of *Space Invaders*, which consisted of one blob at the bottom of the television screen (who is the player) shooting an organised mass of blobs at the top (the space invaders). However, each of the blobs in the organised mass of blobs could drop bomb-type blobs on the player's blob. If the player's blob was bombed three times, the game would end. The player's blob had to shoot every single blob in the organised mass so that they would not descend from space and land on the larger blob that was supposed to be the Earth.

In complete contrast to *Space Invaders* was a 2-player game called *Combat*, which involved one blob on the left of the television screen and another on the right side. Both blobs could fire smaller blobs at each other and any direct hits would score points. I may have only been 12 years old, but I knew that high-resolution pixellation already existed. Needless to say, many years later, Atari went bust.

Unfortunately, my carefully rewritten Presents and Property policy was still in effect in 1987 when my parents bought my brother a Commodore-64 Home Computer as an upgrade to his Atari. The same year, I began to study for my Higher School Certificate (equivalent to A-levels) and was rewarded with Jane Fonda's Workout Video. I called Childline:

Hello, I'd like to report my family to the authorities. You see they're Chinese, which means that my mother's duty, by tradition, is to her father, husband and son. That means they can be charged with my neglect, right? I have evidence to support this. I'm studying for my Higher School Certificate and my brother won't let me use his computer to type my essays. I have my handwritten coursework to prove it! Furthermore, my brother only uses his computer to play games which he can do on his Atari. My purposes are educational, yet my parents won't intervene. My future depends on being able to use the computer and they're trying to sabotage it by giving me Jane Fonda's Workout Video. In 1981, they gave me a wind-up jewellery box. It's a conspiracy to inflict gender stereotypes upon me so that I grow up into a narcissicist who can't spell, thereby increasing my chances of attracting a Chinese accountant husband. I think I have a good case for emotional abuse here, and physical if you count the workout video.

I can't remember how it got resolved, or if it ever did. Now I'm too old to ring Childline, but the skills I acquired from *Combat* and *Space Invaders* have been useful on the front line and in more covert operations when it comes to participating in other technologies.

1996

Somewhere in his youth or childhood, he must have done something good. Or so the bloke demonstrating the software must have thought: to be born male, and therefore to have such licence to speak to me so patronisingly.

Having arrived early, I had the opportunity of witnessing the other participants enter the room and take their seats. Immediately prior to the presentation, I checked the publicity material for any conditions like 'Only white men wearing ill-fitting suits will be admitted.' I made an excuse to go to the ladies' toilet so that I could search for the sign outside I had evidently missed, warning that any woman, particularly one from an ethnic minority, would feel distinctly out of place if any attempt was made to participate in the seminar. Nobody said the life of an Other would be so awkward yet empowering; that to be unlikely – an ethnic minority woman and competent in multimedia technology – was audacious, even threatening.

Perhaps that was why the software being demonstrated was called something akin to HandyTool, reminiscent of men tinkering in garages, just as my own father did.

Surrounded by tools, the garage was a space of invention, where Dad produced, all by himself, an overwhelming conviction that he could build a set of gates for the driveway despite having no experience of building gates or anything for that matter.

'What does this do?' I remember asking my father, pointing to the sander.

'What can't it do?' replied my father, and added 'Don't touch it, it's dangerous.'

When I took my seat again, the HandyTool demonstrator asked me if I was interested in any particular aspect of the software. I stated my position: 'I've never used the software before, so I just want to know basically what it can do.'

'What can't it do?' he replied with a degree of smarm only software salesmen can attain. According to the demonstrator, this constituted an adequate answer and he proceeded to ignore me for the remainder of the presentation. The other participants obviously felt that I had taken up quite enough of his time already with such trivial issues as what the software can do, and so bombarded him with questions about precisely the opposite:

How does this package compare with Producer, which is not only the industry standard, but is capable of shrinking text to such an extent that a 70,000 word book can be printed on half a sheet of A4? It's definitely going to revolutionise the publishing industry. How will HandyTool meet the challenge?

From an educational perspective, I've found Sod The Teacher a remarkable piece of software in that I can produce the next week's lessons when driving home in the car, so that I can come in on a Monday, take the register, load the applications on the computers, have a cup of tea in the staff room and then go home. I don't have to come in for the rest of the week. Does HandyTool have the same educational value?

I've been using the Black & Decker Pneumatic Multimedia Authoring System which not only allows the users to design gates for their driveways, but in the process, simulates the sounds of a construction site as a source of inspiration, and actually will have the gates built for you by contacting the nearest carpenter or welder via its Internet link. Can HandyTool live up to this?

The demonstrator believed in his company's product and his incisive business brain knew that if HandyTool could not perform all these tasks, none of the participants would buy it. When all the questions were exhausted, having been conquered with a baffling combination of acronyms and jargon, the participants left subdued. As they filed out of the room, the demonstrator approached me with a business card: 'I'm sorry if this was all above your head, but here are the details of our female sales executive. Give her a call, she would be happy to answer any questions you have.'

As the last participant was leaving, his comic talents came to the fore as he said to me with great side-splitting hilarity: 'Are you having it all explained again?'

The irony of my Otherness lies in the perverse affinity that technology has given me with The (so-called) Opposition. It is a kind of love-hate relationship that is articulated in sibling rivalry: I hated my brother, but we both loved technology. Ditto for me and other 'techies': despite their conscious or unconscious attempts to exclude me, I declare myself a 'techie'. By being Other and yet one of Them, by polluting the association of technology with masculinity, I am a cyborg.

Technology, tradition and transition: the journey of a middle-class Indian woman

Nanda Bandyopadhyay

I was born at the time India was about to become independent: an era of flux and transformation, a time when established systems of power and ideology were rapidly metamorphosing. During the independence movement many women fought actively against the British Raj. When Gandhi launched the civil disobedience campaign in 1930, the British banned the Indian National Congress (the organisation which co-ordinated the independence movement) and put most of its leaders in jail. At this point women came into their own and took over the organisation of the campaign. This not only raised women's consciousness, it also served to change the attitude of some men who, while not accepting the principle of sexual equality, recognised that supporting women's suffrage was necessary for the nationalist cause (Liddle and Joshi 1988). Though any changes made to the law of the country were often ineffective and, in any case only favoured the middle classes, the perspective of both men and women from these classes began to change through this process. The country was in transition and hope was the order of the day.

One very important aspect of this was the changing attitudes and aspirations of a large number of women who grew up in the environment of the independence movement (late 19th to the mid-20th century). Although the British had not allowed women to enter the new administrative occupations, women began to move into medicine and teaching at the beginning of the 20th century, a move facilitated by the demand for the education and health care of middle-class women which, because of sex segregation and female seclusion, required the service of women (Liddle and Joshi 1988). Such changes exerted a great influence on the ordinary Indian women who had had to accept women's oppression and the restrictions imposed by tradition in their own lives, and, for the first time, were offered role models of women coming out of seclusion to establish their own identities. Although homebound themselves, after independence was declared in August 1947 women became a strong driving force behind the social change that occurred in a now-jubilant India. While Hinduism essentially acknowledged the value of women as life-givers and sources of activating energy, these women were developing the concept of 'women's power' into a set of common cultural assumptions. They utilised their privileged status in the home to bring in change; not only to improve the lives of their daughters but also to mobilise society away from its traditional orthodox ideas. These newly-empowered women included my mother; and the lessons she had learnt from the independence movement informed her tastes, choices and ideology for the rest of her life.

In this chapter I wish to explore how such changes affected typical (sub)urban middle-class families by using memories of my childhood and youth in India. I am not trying to portray the history of a society, nor debate the implications of inequalities between the different classes and genders. Instead, I utilise the history of a real person (me) who, although a minority in the context of the whole country, was a part of the large middle-classes in urban India.

In assessing the research carried out on the sociology of modernisation and development, Harrison (1988) suggests that tradition is often portrayed as a barrier to technological change. Technology is seen as an important element of modernisation; one which negates history, advances civilisation and precludes tradition. In this chapter, I contest this view and present technology as having an important role in tradition as well as in modernity. I do so both by distinguishing between traditional and modern technologies and by emphasising the symbolic, as well as the material, aspects of technologies. Thus, in my account, I show how the use of traditional technologies functioned as sites of resistance against both Eurocentric modernisation in India, and against the threatened negation of my Indian identity when I later came to England. However, the picture is more complex and contradictory than this. As I shall show, I did not experience modern technologies solely as externally-imposed attempts to repress aspects of Indian culture and tradition that I sought to preserve, but also as representing an opportunity for escape from the limitations to personal freedom placed on women by traditional family structures and conventions. In this story of my intellectual and personal journey, I explore the contradictory meanings that technology had for me and my family and friends as we negotiated our identity positions in relation to the tension between the traditional and the modern in Indian society during the decades following independence. In this endeavour, I suggest that my story might be read as a cyborg story.

I grew up in urban Calcutta during the late 40s and early 50s in a traditional, so-called 'joint' family which consisted of my father's two brothers, a widowed sister and their families, as well as some of my father's male cousins (called brothers or 'cousin brothers'). I grew up with my cousins who were close to my age, played on the roof with them and went to the same school as one of them. Joint families were common then; the household expenditure and responsibilities were shared by the brothers but the eldest brother – my father in our case – was treated as the head of the household and had to take extra responsibilities. Thus, whilst the others paid a fixed amount in the household kitty, it was his responsibility to make up any difference caused by inflation or an unexpected expenditure such as a family guest staying for a long period. He was also the head of the family and the others were expected to take his (and/or my mother's) advice on all serious matters. On the other hand, people of each generation had to be respectful and obedient to all those belonging to a higher generation within a wide range of extended family and communal structures.

In 1950, my grandfather had the house built in the suburb of Calcutta close to the international airport. He thought, as did other people who moved into that area, that this was far enough from the city to be quiet and close enough to the airport to be 'developed' in future. My grandfather bought a lot of land. Even at a young age I was aware of the legacy of British rule and the effect it had on some Indians' notions of modernity and civilisation. Next to our house lived a 'Raybahadur' (a title given to obedient Indians by the British) who had bought a bungalow built by the British together with servants' quarters, gardens and a garage over a large area. They had a car and a chauffeur, a piano for the women in the family (they played Western classical music), a badminton court in the lawn, a fridge and many other things that we found both attractive and strange. This mixture of reactions to the signifiers of Western 'civilisation' not only

LIVERPOOL JOHN MOORES UNIVERSITY
LEARNING SERVICES

typified my later attitude to my life in England, it also emphasised the class differences between my family and that of our neighbour. They were classed as rich and we belonged to the middle class, which in the Indian context meant middle income people with jobs (as opposed to businesses) whose lives centred round keeping their families safe and healthy and giving their children an education which would equip them to earn a living. Such families managed to survive reasonably if they planned well but had little money in the bank; whatever they had in the form of insurance policies and so on were meant for sudden illnesses or daughters' weddings. However, we were considered rich by many people in various degrees of poverty: those who earned very little and had a large family to support, those who lived on casual and unskilled work, the domestic servants who earned enough to have very basic food but had little left for anything else, and finally those who earned nothing and lived by begging. In other words, the situation was not really very different from how it is in contemporary England.

While I was growing up, our use of technology reflected such relative positions of privilege and status in society. Even at this early stage in post-independent India's history, there was a marked split between the technology of tradition and technology of modernity, between British 'sophistication' and Indian 'resourcefulness' and 'innovation'. Whilst our rich neighbour had a shower in the bathroom, a bath tub and a sink as well as an electric pump to get 24-hour running water, we used a deep well in our back garden and a pulley system to dip in a bucket to fetch clean drinking water. In our bathroom we had a built-in tank on the floor with a tap connected to the water supply and a little hole at the bottom to empty it for cleaning. The tank got filled up when municipality water came through the taps twice or three times a day; we had to use a small bucket to pour water over ourselves standing on the concrete floor to have a bath. On days off school my two cousins and I used to get into the bathroom together and sit inside the water tank for fun. Needless to say this un-hygienic act was performed without the knowledge of our elders who had to use the same water for their bath. Poor people often had no private water supply; they had to depend on a public tubewell or a tap for fresh water. This, in a country where personal hygiene is very important (one of the reasons for this is that you have to be clean before you make your daily offering to religious deities), meant there were always queues in front of these water supplies.

My grandfather spent most of his time in his village home where his ancestors settled in six generations before. Ours was one of the rich families in the village; my great grandfather was a doctor and also had a lot of land in the village which created a large income. Although quite progressive as a family (they built the first boys' and then the girls' schools in the village which are large now and still bear their names), my grandfather was, like many people of his generation and social status, proud of his tradition and did not want modern technology in the house. Instead he imported a number of traditional technologies from his village home: the well in our back garden was one of those, as was the cowshed, where we had a cow, and a milkman came morning and afternoon to get fresh milk for us.

As youngsters, we saw many disadvantages of 'tradition' and especially of the burden of having to share our hopes and dreams with the extended family. We had many elders to obey and many traditional rules to accept. For example, our parents were not allowed to demonstrate any special affection to us in public. In describing the patrifocal practices and structures in Indian society, Subrahmanyan suggests that: '[i]ndividuals are expected to subordinate their goals and interests to that of the family in general and extended family specifically, regardless of the way the household is set up' (1998: 39). We couldn't have any modern Western-style amenities or 'luxuries' that other households were purchasing, such as sinks and showers instead of tanks, and gas instead of the smokey coal fire for cooking. We resented the way such a structure held us back (or so we thought) from becoming 'modern': collective life made it difficult for us to formulate or realise any distinct personal ambitions.

The joint family system enabled middle income families to enjoy some communal luxuries, such as having full time servants and cooks, or a large house to live in, but often deprived its members of personal indulgence. We did not own any (commercial) toys because anything our parents wanted to buy for us they also had to buy for our cousins. My concept of 'traditional technology' was formed by our own childish resourcefulness. For entertainment, we had to innovate by making dolls out of old material and beds for them out of boxes. We owned a big garden and we made a swing by tying a rope to the branches of a tree. Poorer children entertained themselves in similar ways, only they had to find a public tree to build a swing or find the wheel trim of an old bicycle and a stick to roll it with. Innovation is a way of life in a poor country; it is how a fifty year old car is kept on the road in a climate where weather and environmental pollution take their toll. However, things changed rapidly within a few years. Whilst my sister and I had to be satisfied with home-made items, my brother, who was born nine years after me, had a cradle which used to hang from the ceiling in my parents' bedroom, and a tricycle when he was older. There were two reasons for these differences between us. First he was the son my parents longed for; and second, when he was quite young we moved out of the joint family in search of modernisation, and this allowed my mother to indulge in some luxuries for her children (the tricycle was a small symbol of that). Thus, while I had to rely on home-made, traditional technology in my childhood, my brother benefited from my mother's newly-acquired freedom and the taste of the modern world in the form of commercially-made toys. This encapsulates my technological terminology: the traditional ingenuities which were born of financial limitation and the double-edged 'benefit' of modern technology, which put an end to such creativity even though it also signalled our family's greater wealth.

However, innovation in technology was not merely a matter of childish enjoyment. As a young girl I witnessed one disturbing experience of such innovation by a desperate human being. He was one of my cousins who lived with us; he was much older than me and he committed suicide. He obviously wanted a quick and sure death, so he wrapped one end of an electric cable round his hand and threw the other end from a hanging veranda on to a telegraph pole on a rainy day. I was at school at the time and only saw the line of burnt flesh on his hand when I was summoned to say goodbye before he was taken away for cremation. In a society where sex before marriage was unthinkable he somehow managed to get syphilis. So, when his elders arranged his marriage, he chose to die rather than seek treatment (which was easily available then) in the fear of being found out, or of ruining the life of a woman.

Modern domestic technology was not easily available in those days, mainly because, in contravention of the grand myth of Western civilisation and progress, it was not seen as necessary or viable. The country's priority was agriculture and technological development concentrated on tractors, rotation of crops and building dams. In a country where labour is cheap and a large number of people depend on domestic jobs, there is little demand for domestic technology. Even now, when many everyday labour-saving devices are available, few people buy them because it is cheaper and more convenient to employ a servant to do the work. Furthermore, the inventions of the modern world do not necessarily refine or improve traditional technologies. There are some old forms of technology which cannot be replaced by new ones, and these are part of the 'traditional technological' schema I have defined above. For example, spices are ground everyday by putting them on a thick, rough and flat oval-shaped slab of stone, mixing them with water and pressed using backward and forward movements with another long and cylindrical stone. An electrical grinder simply does not produce the same result. People do not use knives in the kitchen but a sharp and curved metal blade stuck on a piece of flat wood at a right-angle. The user sits on the floor with it and puts one leg on the wood to keep it steady and cuts with both hands. I know Indian people living in England who have brought some of this traditional domestic technology back from home. I still use a sweeper made of long and very thin sticks to sweep my beds and mattresses, a technique used in India to get rid of dust and bed-mites. Every time I go home, I bring back various items of 'old' technology such as a traditional mortar and pestle made of brass which I use instead of a grinder; deep and round cooking pots uniquely suited for Indian cookery; and a special type of heavy tongs for holding hot cooking pots.

As already mentioned, when I was 12, we moved from our extended family home to a government residence given to my father by his employers to join the growing population of nuclear families. This was in the southern part of Calcutta which has always been regarded as very cosmopolitan. Suddenly we were at a point where my parents could pay attention to their aspirations for their children and I had to start taking some responsibilities for my future. This was the time when my mother, one of those women inspired by women's progress during the independence movement, found the opportunity to follow her dreams.

I was quite a serious-minded child. This, together with the general acceptance amongst our relatives that I was ugly because I was dark, had big teeth and light eyes, meant that I had to do well because it would not be easy to find a husband for me and therefore I needed to have a career. This fitted well with my desire to become self-sufficient and my mother's passion for education for her children. Where most females were directed towards 'soft' humanities-based subjects, I had a great passion for maths and science, and was lucky to garner the full support of my family in following my dreams. I was the first female in our extended family circle to be awarded a postgraduate qualification in science. I made my grandfather (actually my grandfather's younger brother, who, in the Indian system, was my grandfather too) proud. He was a lifelong freedom fighter and spent most of his young life in jails. He believed that women should have the same opportunities in education as men and when I received my postgraduate degree in physics he celebrated by presenting me with a bound picture of the social reformer and Nobel-laureate in literature, Tagore.

My mother had many dreams at the root of which was her passion for 'breaking the mould'. She was the driver of my transition towards self-development, and nurtured my instincts to enter areas into which few females ventured. Unlike the other parents who sent their children to dance and music classes, my mother encouraged me to take up physical activities and I joined the National Cadet Corps, which was compulsory for all boys' schools and available in all girls' schools in India at that time (this being the time of the Indo-China war). I learnt to shoot a rifle (and proved to be very good at it), to put up a tent, to fold my bedding in a way that took the least space and was the quickest to open up again, to read a map, to understand Morse code. This was an empowering experience; for the first time in my life I went on a 10-day camp and stayed away from my family, was able to take leadership in my role as a corporal in our group, wore boots and trousers, was taught to walk heels first, learnt to salute, and generally do things previously allowed only to men. However, having done all these things at school, when I walked through the neighbourhood to come home in my uniform (having been dropped by the school bus at the top of our lane), I had to put up with teasing comments from young men standing at the street corner for their regular social gathering!

My mother's support of female self-advancement was also borne out in the home: it was I who performed household tasks usually left to boys. I had to fiddle with the wiring in the little box connecting the telephone when it did not work, and wire plugs when new electrical items were bought. I was also made to do other little jobs at home like painting and putting a nail in the wall, a difficult job given the brick walls of Indian buildings and the tools of hammer, chisel and putty. I never cooked. Instead, my job at home was to help my brother with his maths and science. My father would tutor him for English and other subjects and call me when he got stuck with the technical matters.

However, the stigma surrounding careers suitable for women was strong.

It was believed that working in an office was 'common' and that academia was the only suitable profession for middle-class women. College lectureship was seen as a 'respectable' job for a woman until an offer for marriage comes along. In India 'middle class women may work outside the home, but there are still criteria of respectability to be upheld ... the respectability can be upheld by restricting women's sexual freedom in the job, and through emphasising the economic and status benefits attaching to her occupation' (Liddle and Joshi 1988: 108).

Nonetheless, it gave me an immense sense of achievement to advance in a field usually reserved for men, and as part of my drive towards my ambitions I tried to enter the computing profession. India's first computer was installed at the Indian Statistical Institute (ISI) in 1955. By 1965 there were 16 computer centres in the country (Singhal and Rogers 1989). Most of these were used for research and development and in education. By 1972, there were 175 computer systems nationwide, 75% of which were IBM. Some of the computer centres (such as ISI) ran courses in computer programming. India, known world-wide as a poor and apparently backward country, was disproportionately ahead in technology. The mood was one of optimism as we attempted to crest the silicon boom. However, it did not work out for me for logistical reasons and I started my working life teaching physics to undergraduate women.

On the other hand, having high qualifications in science and being a working woman, especially one who had to live away from home to do so (as well as being ugly), made me less eligible for marriage. The stigma against unmarried women was even stronger than that against office-working women, and since I had been brought up believing in my lack of physical beauty I was vulnerable on this point. Even my usually indomitable mother got rather worried that I would stay an old maid all my life. She wanted her daughter to be smart and an individual but she found the embarrassment of having an unmarried daughter, and one who may end up supporting her parents in their old age, frightening. In the climate in which I grew up, a woman had a large amount of freedom to choose her career, hobbies and cultural activities up to a certain age, after which traditions, family honour and social pressures stepped in. Although theoretically free to do what we wanted, the indirect pressure to conform, combined with a deep-rooted sense of responsibility and a real fear of ending up by ourselves and being pitied by the rest of the society, prevented most of us from remaining unmarried. Although some of my friends survived the pressure and stayed single, most of us talked ourselves into believing that a career can be maintained after wedlock. The extended family structure in India, which went beyond the confines of relatives into the neighbourhoods and communities, resulted in young people growing up with an unnecessary, excessive regard for elders and authorities. Additionally, social pressures were always more acute on middle class women than their lower or upper class counterparts. Thus, I accepted a proposal of marriage and came to England in 1973 with the confidence that my knowledge of science and technology would enable me to survive in what I suspected might be a hostile environment.

India is an elitist society and education plays an important role. Parents work hard to ensure that their children can maintain, and, if possible, improve their position in society. My education promised me survival in such a world and gave me credibility in my search for employment even after I came to England. However, it also gave me a false sense of security. Although empowered and modern in my outlook and education, the most trifling simplicities of 'modern technology' provided me with ample opportunity for embarrassment. When I first came to this country many consumer goods which people here took for granted were new to me and ended up being the reasons for humiliation. For example, I once worked as an information scientist in a large company that produced toiletries. We received free samples of their fabric conditioner and, not knowing what it was, I used it to wash clothes. Naturally it did not work, but when I, very naively, described my experience to one of my colleagues (as a funny story, I thought), she ridiculed me to her friends. My reality had led me to feel superior to this woman because she had five 'O' levels when I had an MSc in physics. Only a racist society would employ both of us for a job which required a science graduate. I felt my social and academic background put me above such ridicule; the other woman obviously thought differently. It did not matter that I knew about the viscosity of shampoo and she didn't; what was important in this situation was that she knew what a fabric conditioner was and I didn't. My many years of scientific study and my dedicated journey towards learning had been undermined by my failure to recognise that great advance in Western shirt-washing practices, the fabric conditioner!

Suddenly I was forced into a margin from where I had to reassess my modernity. I used 'my' technology again; I finally got into computing, initially as a programmer, and eventually as a lecturer in a further education college. In the college I had a boss who considered himself a foreigner (he was a Scot), had a strong accent, a very deep sense of roots, a well-known temper, an understanding of integrity, respect for different cultures and a refusal to take any bullshit. With his support, I made progress. I also did a master's in computer science and eventually took over his job some time after he retired. Although I was accepted, affectionately, by many people who got to know me, I gained a reputation as one with a 'bit of a nose' from male scientists and engineers in the college who found it hard to accept a little Indian woman with personality. Gradually I gathered confidence in my identity as an Indian woman who fitted in but did not always subscribe to the dominant culture and I managed to make further progress in my career. I found comfort through my yearly visit home (by now, I could afford it) with increasing appreciation of the traditional extended family and community structure while realistically accepting what the Western modernity could offer me when I came back – recharged.

In these short autobiographical reflections I have mapped out a series of episodes in which notions of tradition, enlightenment, progress and modernity seem to have been in perpetual flux. As a child and young woman in India, the technology of modern science had been something that set me apart and gave me status as a woman entering new fields of intellectual study and development, yet it was also one route to be followed by a woman who was traditionally not considered marriageable. My progressive mother wanted me to have the best education available, but this route also isolated me as a woman in a traditionally male-dominated field, and reflected the narrow possibilities for women at the time. The technology of modernity, as defined by Western progress and invention, offered me the chance to go to England, expecting that my high qualifications would aid my integration with British working life, but it also brought me into conflict with the cultural assumptions I encountered there. At the same time, I cherished those symbols of traditional technology which recalled the necessary resourcefulness of my childhood.

I eventually reconciled myself with a Westernised version of modern technology, using technology as a weapon in this world of contradictions, oppressions and opportunities. I made a point of never forgetting where I came from and what principles my background had instilled in me – the importance of family ties, of education, of women's empowerment – yet also embraced everything the 'modern' world had to offer, maintaining a profile in a technology-centric job. Thus throughout my life I have experienced first-hand the interdependence and permeability of tradition, modernity, patriarchy, colonialism and technology (Graham 1999), endorsing Haraway's observation of a cyborg world in which identity is cultivated through permanently partial and oscillating histories and simultaneous contradictory standpoints. In keeping both the traditional and the modern always in play in my own life, I construct myself as having a cyborgian identity.

Section 3

Resisting the cyborg life?

I'd rather be a goddess than a cyborg: technobiographical tales, from drains to divas

Nod Miller

I N this chapter I describe and analyse some aspects of my technobiographical journey, a trajectory which leads me to the provisional conclusion that the metaphor of the goddess provides a more helpful and aesthetically appealing model than that of the cyborg for understanding my orientation towards technology. The key technologies on which I focus in my narrative are those of plumbing and popular music reproduction.

When the technobiographies project began in 1996, I had already spent some years mining my memory, subjectivity and life history for research purposes. I had written and published academic texts which incorporated auto/biographical stories. Technology was largely absent from these narratives, although I was aware of the impact of my developing familiarity with word-processing software on my own process of academic text production, and the accounts of adult education practice which I contributed to the research literature on learning and teaching (exemplified in Miller 1993a and b) reflected my interests in the use of mass media technologies such as television and the press for educational purposes.

Beginning with the plumbing

Here is an extract from my first attempt at technobiography:

Dreams of working bathrooms
Many of my childhood memories connected with items of technology are tied to non-possession or deprivation. The concept of deprivation was not

one I articulated as a child, although I was conscious that arguments between my parents were usually about money, and that their discussions about the acquisition of new possessions were generally tense and anxious. Here I focus on some recollections from childhood on the way in which relationships in the household revolved around items of domestic hardware. I was born in 1949 and grew up in an extended working-class family in Kidderminster, a small industrial town in the West Midlands (of England). My parents possessed neither a car nor a telephone (items without which my present lifestyle would be unthinkable), and for at least one day a week my mother's time was taken up with washing and drying the household laundry. My early recollections of this activity are of a complex and dangerous ritual, as there were no washing machines or dryers, and washing and rinsing water needed to be brewed up in the large and noisy copper boiler which occupied a prominent place in the back scullery of our house. The boiling of water in the copper was also a necessary procedure for the weekly bathing of persons. Although my parents' house, which was then owned by my grandparents, incorporated a bathroom (situated off the front parlour or 'dining room' which was only used on special occasions), there was no direct water supply in that part of the house, so that it was necessary to boil water in the back kitchen and to carry buckets of water through the downstairs rooms of the house and pour them into the bath. Several refills of the copper were necessary to meet the needs of bath night (which was Friday night in my early childhood, but which later shifted to Sunday). Carrying the pails of water was one of the few household tasks which was not gender-specific. Naturally enough, several members of the household were obliged to share the same bath water, and I was accustomed to sharing space in the bath with my mother until the approach of my teens.

I was probably at secondary school before I became aware that the organisation of bath time as was customary in my home was not part of a universal pattern. Although I didn't have a sophisticated theory of social class at that time, I was aware of my own family's place in a complex set of class and status relations. Clearly we were less posh than lots of the girls with whom I became acquainted at grammar school, who lived in houses with bathrooms which had working plumbing. On the other hand, several of my friends in the road lived in small terraced houses with outside lavatories and communal washhouses. The toilets, too, were communal, with long wooden seats with two or three holes in them, allowing visits to the toilet to be conducted in companionable fashion. My own house did have an inside lavatory — two, in fact — but most of the time neither worked very well. The roof in the upstairs lavatory leaked badly whenever it rained, and the door had warped, making it impossible to shut it completely. One of my aunts who visited the house at intervals would joke about how going to the toilet in our house involved sitting with an umbrella in one hand to keep off the rainwater while keeping one leg jammed up against the door to repel unwanted visitors and singing loudly to warn them off. There was no lighting on the upstairs landing or in the toilet, so that visiting the lavatory at night was a hazardous business. Chamber pots under beds were standard equipment, while the succession of elderly relatives who stayed in the house during my childhood (several of whom died there after periods of illness) used commodes in the bedrooms. I formed the impression early on that my mum spent a lot of her time emptying and cleaning chamber pots, and I think my perceptions of the domestic division of labour, with the disposal of urine and faeces being classified as women's work, probably contributed to the formation of my view (expressed when I first went to school) that I didn't want to get married.

I wrote this fragment in January 1997, when I was still quite new to innovation studies, and, reading this text four years later, I am aware of the assumption embedded in this story that technology is represented by objects. These days I am accustomed to thinking of technology in social constructionist terms. Nevertheless, my conception of and interest in technology still revolve around things and I continue to be intrigued by the way in which identities and memories are inscribed in the material.

This story reflects the continuing preoccupations I have with the way in which technologies are tied up with identity and status. The idea of technologies being differentiated in terms of their associations with either women's or men's work has been part of my taken-for-granted reality for a long time, and the symbolic significance of technological items in conveying status or social class position featured in my earliest attempts to make sense of the social world.

Contextualising the story

Dreams of working bathrooms was shaped in part by two aspects of the context in which I wrote the piece. The first concerned the building in which members of the Technobiographies Group worked, where running water and lavatories were two floors away from where most of us had our offices. Dealing with everyday matters such as washing up and toilet needs gave rise to some inconvenience, and the unwashed detritus of coffee breaks and picnic lunches which often littered the staff room served as reminders of the importance of technologies such as plumbing, which in modern buildings tend to be taken entirely for granted. Our debates about digital technologies in the Department were sometimes interspersed with wry observations about the primitive technological state of the physical surroundings where we conducted our intellectual deliberations.

Another plumbing preoccupation of mine at that time arose from the fact I wrote the bathrooms piece in a house which lacked a properly functioning bathroom. For some months my home had been the subject of the ministrations of a succession of builders who dismantled the second floor of the house in order to install a new bathroom complete with space capsule shower and two-person Jacuzzi bath. When at last the work was complete, I bathed in the grandeur of the shiny new equipment and reflected on the social mobility which it signified. I wondered to what extent my anxiety to acquire top-of-the-range sanitaryware and to have a bathroom to my precise specifications reflected my early deprivation in this area of my life.

One of my first jobs after I graduated in 1970 involved selling bathroom equipment in the showroom of a Kidderminster plumbers' merchant. I knew nothing about the technical aspects of bathroom installation, but learned sufficient of the restricted code of the sanitary engineers to bluff my way through sales negotiations. In the process I developed a taste for exotic taps, extravagently large baths and power showers. At that time, midnight blue, aubergine and avocado baths and basins were hyper-trendy. I did not appreciate then that these shades were magnets for limescale and thus extremely difficult to clean. I found this out when I moved into a house which had been equipped with dream bathroom kit in the now naff 1970s. This equipment was ripped out so that my own bathroom dream could be realised.

I found it difficult to analyse my perceptions about plumbing – both in the 1950s and the 1990s – in terms of the metaphors with which the Technobiographies Group played in our collective attempts to locate ourselves in relation to technological objects and processes. When we discussed our technological identities and whether we saw ourselves as inside or outside or all mixed up with technologies, I had difficulty in stuffing my thoughts and selves into a fixed location. When we started to conceptualise our collective exploration as an analysis of cyborgian experience, my plumbing stories still failed to fit.

However confused I was about my location in relation to digital technologies, I was clear that there were some types of tools and processes from which I was happy to keep a distance. In the course of replumbing the house, our builders unearthed all sorts of sordid sights and smells and I learned more than I wanted to about pipes and flushing systems and macerators and what happened when they came apart or malfunctioned. I had no desire whatever to be 'at one' with this kind of technology (to borrow a phrase from Helen Kennedy's endearing account of her perception of a colleague during her technofraud days). The thought of being a cyborg with plumbing components was quite repellent.

Encountering Pallas Athene

Helen, Linda Leung and I worked together on an action research initiative during 1996 to 1998 which we labelled Project @THENE. The acronym stood for Accessing Technology for Higher Education and New Enterprise, with the then relatively novel @ sign signifying our confident grasp of new technological discourse. Supported by a development grant from British Telecommunications plc and working with a neighbouring community provider of women's education and training, we devised and implemented a part-distance foundation course in technology studies for women returning to study. The course made use of the multimedia technologies which formed a large part of the curriculum content as the mode of course delivery, and it recruited an ethnically diverse group of women, whose learning about cyber-identities underpins some of the analysis in other chapters of this book.

We worked hard at the @THENE acronym. It seemed apt in the context of a feminist project to use the name of a goddess. We came up with Athene, the name of the Greek goddess who turned out to have technology, wisdom and women's crafts (as well as war) in her extensive portfolio. The promotional video which we made for Project @THENE featured a representation of Pallas Athene, fetchingly equipped with traditional helmet, shield and sword (or was it a *Star Wars* light sabre?), pointing assertively at pieces of kit with her weapon to make them spring into action. She didn't look much like a woman who tangled too closely with the innards of a PC. In certain respects, she was like me. Although I was styled 'project director' of @THENE, early on in the course of the project I resigned myself to having to defer to the technical knowledge of multimedia possessed by colleagues who were my juniors (at least in age), and I came to rely heavily on their skills. As I became further acquainted with the digital world of the mid-1990s, I began to feel my age.

For much of my professional career as a media educator, the tools of my trade had tended to be associated with the activities of boffins or nerds. All of a sudden nerds had started to become street-credible. I also became aware of a casual ageism which seemed to operate on parts of the electronic superhighway. The protagonist of Generation X novelist Douglas Coupland's *Microserfs* is 26 years old and clearly sees Silicon Valley as a place for the young and cool. He enjoys working at Nintendo 'where everybody's just a bit younger and hipper than at Microsoft ... Everyone at Microsoft seems, well, literally 31.2 years old, and it shows.' (1996: 15). I could not hope to compete in the cyberchick stakes, or emulate the cyberstyle exemplified by Helen and Linda (see Kennedy in this volume). But, heaven knows, being (or perhaps more accurately constructing myself as) a goddess seemed no uncomfortable thing. My wardrobe (predominantly Issey Miyake, with accessories by Prada and Manolo Blahnik) fits more gracefully with ageing hippy goddess aspirant than with the hard-edged, metallic half-woman, half-mouse which the cyborg image brings to mind.

Constructing the technobiographical self

As members of the Technobiographies Group crafted and honed their first-person accounts of their technological lives, others in the Group attempted meta-analyses which would contribute to the development of theory from the stories of experience. A subgroup of which I was part produced a series of texts from which the introductory chapter to this book was developed. One of my interests in this group was in the way that we constructed ourselves (our selves?) in the auto/biographical stories. At some point during 1997, I fantasised about the film or television shows which might be made from our stories, and I wrote a series of pitches for these treatments. I conceptualised Sally Wyatt's story of her upbringing in the shadow of the power station as a haunting family drama financed by the

National Film Board of Canada and featuring Cher, John Travolta and Quentin Tarantino in key roles. Helen Kennedy's narrative was transposed to New York and developed as a *Friends*-style sitcom, while Gwyneth Hughes's account of her formative years in the chemistry lab was translated into a romantic comedy thriller featuring k.d.lang and Ellen de Generes. Here is part of my pitch, based on the autobiographical fragment which incorporated the plumbing story as well as descriptions of the technology of the drop-forgings factory where my father worked. There are also references to earlier writings which reflect my interests in C. Wright Mills's sociological imagination (see Miller 1993b), and in the 'animation' of learning from experience (Boud and Miller 1996). 'My life and bookshelves' was the title of an autobiographical chapter in my PhD thesis (1993b).

This Saturday Night Life

A flashy red open-top MG disturbs the somnolence of a West Midlands mill town one Sunday morning. NOD has been drawn inescapably back to her home town to search out the mysterious connection in her life with the shadowy figure of C WRIGHT MILLS. But as she drives past the scenes of her childhood, we see in flashback some of the formative incidents in her life, including the strange case of next door's outside toilet, and the Drop Forgings From Hell. As NOD pieces together the puzzle that connects her life and bookshelves we begin to understand the difference between animation and facilitation.

In this Boulting Brothers production, the contemporary NOD is played by Marianne Faithfull; the younger NODs are played by Meg Ryan and Alicia Silverstone. Peggy Ashcroft and John Mills star as NOD'S PARENTS and ALAN, NOD's brother, is played by Sting. Donald Sutherland appears in a cameo as DICK, NOD's ex-husband. C WRIGHT MILLS is played by Eddie Izzard.

The pitches which I produced represented a game which I have played at intervals throughout my life – or at least since I discovered the concept of 'life scripts' (Berne 1973) in a course on transactional analysis which I undertook in 1973. This game addresses the following questions: if I were producing a film of *The Nod Miller Story*, in what genre would it be located? Which events would form pivotal points in the narrative? Who would be cast in the central roles? Would the audience laugh, cry, or want its money back? (I invariably choose contemporary cultural icons with touches of the goddess to represent me; this theme is developed further in Miller 2000.)

Taking apart the soundtrack

Before too long in the process of media production which my autobiographical narratives have become, the issue of what to include in the soundtrack arises. I write this sentence, as I write almost all my sentences, to the accompaniment of rock music CDs. Here my track of the moment is *Rhiannon*, Stevie Nicks's melodramatic hymn to a Welsh witch from the 1975 album *Fleetwood Mac*.

So let me consider now the composition of the soundtrack of *This Saturday Night Life*. The starting point implied in the film treatment is that of a car journey, so perhaps an in-car audio cassette of Jackson Browne's *Running on Empty* (1977) would set the right tone for this version of the Heroine's Journey (as described by writers such as Vogler 1996). In the early 1980s I owned an MG, although it was hard-top and dark green rather than a red convertible. So back I go to the small town where I was born, on an exploration of past selves and relationships. Perhaps I am returning to Kidderminster, as I did in 1999, for my father's funeral. His death provoked not just grief and depression but also a sharp insight into the way in which the narratives of popular culture are woven tightly into my subjectivity. Memories of my dad provide a cue for some snatches of a Bing Crosby song – perhaps his duet with Frank Sinatra, *Well Did You Evah?* from *High Society*.

My father has a lot to answer for in socialising me into a lifetime habit of pop music. We might not have been able to afford central heating or even running water in the bathroom, but nothing stopped my dad from buying weekly fixes of music (or indeed from chain smoking: another aspect of his legacy with which I struggle). The first records I remember were my dad's 78s. He had every song by Bing Crosby, the Old Groaner, that he was able to track down, and that is a lot of tracks. At the end of his life, my dad was blind and hence required audio translations of lists of lyrics on CD reissues of Bing's greatest hits. He remained as enthusiastic as ever for record shopping, and visits to London afforded opportunities to search for esoteric morsels in HMV or the Virgin Megastore. My mother regularly read out the title of every track in every rack in every aisle which offered access to the music and memories of their youth and only very occasionally lost her temper.

The first 33rpm record our family ever owned (*A Christmas Sing with Bing*) was ruined when one of us attempted to play it on a wind-up gramophone with needles like thick steel nails. Some of my earliest childhood memories are of weekly trips to Wilson's, Kidderminster's one music shop. Much of its space was devoted to displays of sheet music, but at some point in the 1950s it adjusted its stock to take account of changing tastes in home entertainment. One of my favourite activities became that of listening to the latest pop record releases in booths installed in Wilson's, equipped with huge bakelite earphones.

The first record I ever bought myself was a 45rpm single – *Return to Sender* by Elvis Presley, in 1962 or thereabouts. 45s could be played over and over if the arm over the turntable was left up, which enabled me to memorise the lyrics of every favourite song as well as every musical nuance. Few of the formal educational lessons I learned at this time are imprinted in my brain in the way that the lyrics of The Crickets, Ketty Lester, The Platters, Bobby Darin or even Cliff Richard are. The first album I owned was Bob Dylan's *Highway 61 Revisited* (1966), although Dad bought all the Beatles albums up to *Revolver* the day they came out. I started building up a serious 33rpm collection towards the end of my undergraduate days. Records from this period have inner sleeves inscribed with sentimental messages from former boyfriends. No doubt those of my contemporaries who took care of their collections, brushing individual records with furry cleaners and never failing to replace them carefully in the correct sleeves, have cleaned up in the current market for cult vinyl. However, the crowd I hung out with treated these important objects with little more regard for their remaining pristine as those inventive people of the 1950s who advocated moulding old 78s into flower holders. Many of my records bear the battle scars of late nights, lost weekends and heated arguments.

Despite my early determination to avoid matrimony, I bowed to tradition in my twenties. My former husband came into our relationship with very few possessions apart from a reel-to-reel tape recorder. We had fun making compilations of favourite rock tracks, interspersed with ethnomethodological banter (I should stage this episode in the style of *Seinfeld* if I included it in my filmic production) on the cumbersome tape machine until it was stolen when the house we shared with three other twenty-somethings was burgled. We threw away the tapes when we left the house. Dick Miller was and I believe still is a dead ringer for Donald Sutherland in his *M*A*S*H* persona, hence the inevitability of the casting above.

The mid-seventies was the era of tape. A friend of that time was very proud of the 8-track stereo he had installed in his Vauxhall Victor (with fins). I thought that the way this machine endlessly described a loop around the tracks of an album was a magical property. The lumpy square cartridges which constituted the software of the period are so exotic and so redolent of their age that they may well pop up soon on *The Antiques Roadshow*. They illustrate perfectly for me the power of technological objects to embody social and personal history.

Most of us moved swiftly to the small plastic c90 tapes which have lasted, for some at least, until this side of the millennium. I have an increasingly raspy collection of compilation tapes from this period to which I still sing along in my car in order to wallow in nostalgia or to conduct auto/biographical research. Throughout the 1970s and '80s, much of the social exchange in my subcultural group was conducted through the exchange of audio cassettes, often painstakingly and lovingly compiled.

Since my early married life was marked by a degree of economic deprivation, Dick and I had to plan our record consumption with some care. But at least we had a bathroom which was relatively modern. My ex plundered the public library for records which were transferred to cassettes, which acquired enhanced value as currency once in-car entertainment in the form of tape machines became standard. When I bought my first sports car (the racy limited-edition MG) the item that clinched the sale was a satisfyingly solid Blaupunkt stereo.

In 1989 I was given a CD player and started buying my record collection all over again. I have so far been given only one compilation CD-R: a collection of cult hits from 1970, the year when I first met the donor. Long ago I gave up any thoughts of conducting research on youth subcultures through participation observation, but I assume that CD burners and minidiscs are essential accoutrements (along with text-messaging Nokias) for the acquisition of social capital in the competitive youth market.

Being a goddess in a cyborg's lair

The room in which I write this chapter could pass for a cyborg's lair. As I write this chapter on my blueberry iMac, I am surrounded by Zip drive, scanner, modem, two telephones, remote-control CD player, Grateful Dead wrist rests, dead cassette players, floppy disks of many diameters including 5.25″ PC and 3″ Amstrad, a television set, dozens of VHS cassettes and hundreds of CDs. And if the 'preferred technology' of cyborgs is writing, then my study bears the hallmarks of a life spent entwined in texts. A rough calculation of the books-per-shelf ratio in my cyborgian environment suggest that I have around 6,000 volumes in this room alone.

Almost invariably my first action when I sit down at my workstation is to switch on the CD player with the remote, which often gets lost in a pile of memos and chapter drafts. I always leave the last CD in the player and the repeat listening to the track where I left off is a comfortingly familiar ritual. I rarely listen to my musical selections via headphones (although I do own at least three Walkpersons and a portable CD player), but the image of the woman-made-cyborg through the stereo headphones clamped to her ears is one representation with which it is possible for me to identify. The operation of needle on vinyl, tape head on oxide or laser beam on CD transports me temporarily (temporally?) to other selves, buried memories and dormant emotions. Much of my autobiographical history is inscribed in the grooves and digits of these little silver discs.

Clearly, although my preference is to approach plumbing technology more in the spirit of Pallas Athene than in that of Haraway's (1985) construction of subjectivity tied up in valves and circuits, the nature of my preferred relationship with music technology is more complex. The preceding brief snapshots of my journey through five decades of consumption of music (and other media) technologies are evidence of this relationship. These were inspired by an experience in the middle of the technobiogaphies project which, I have to acknowledge, had cyborg elements. It also implicates a couple of rock goddesses. Here I open my diary for 1997 for some more flashbacks (falsebacks, I typed there), this time located in California.

Using media technologies for remembrance of relationships past

In the summer of 1997 an incident which occurred while I was on holiday in the USA set me off on a new exploration through technological narratives. A chance encounter with a video biography of a favourite rock band on a cable television channel in California gave rise to recollections of my life and loves of 1977, when the album on which the programme was based was first released. From this experience my exploration developed of the ways in which the changing technologies of music consumption intersect with personal history, emotions, subcultural identity and memory. At the time I described this incident in the following way:

8 August 1997, Palm Springs, California.—Last night I was flicking through the 60-plus channels of cable television available in our rented condo and happened on the image of a musician at a mixing desk describing and explaining the recording and production of a song which he had written. A few bars into the number and my attention was captured. I was back in the 1970s. The musician was Lindsey Buckingham, lead guitarist with Fleetwood Mac, and the programme (in the *Classic Albums* series) told the story of the making of *Rumours,* a record released in 1977 which became one of the best-selling albums of all time, and which was a significant part of the backcloth of my personal history in the late 1970s.

This morning I woke up with tracks from the album playing over and over in my head. As I lay by the pool in the baking desert heat, it felt as if the songs from *Rumours* were tattooed on my brain. Scenes from my life at the time when I first heard the album were being projected onto the back of my eyelids.

In 1977 I was in the second year of my PhD studies in the University of Leicester. I was researching the coverage of educational issues in the British mass media. For most of the time I wallowed in guilt about how little progress I was making with my studies. I rationalised this in part by reference to the turbulent state of my marriage. Some time during 1977 I embarked on a series of entanglements which led me into a shifting pattern of bohemian living arrangements. My marital home was near the university in an area where lots of other graduate students and twenty-something academics lived, and some of them became my close friends. Many of them were also going through separation and divorce at this time and some of them were having affairs with one another. Sometimes pairs or groups of us went shopping or to the cinema together, but most of our social life consisted of sitting around in each others' houses talking about our angst-ridden relationships and listening to rock music. An album which was played over and over on all our turntables was *Rumours* by Fleetwood Mac. The bitter words and combative mood of songs such as *Go your own way* and

Dreams seemed to resonate with my own emotions and relationships.

At least I think that was how it was. As I drifted in and out of consciousness back in Palm Springs I wished I had a personal stereo to hand and I tried to remember what I knew about the musicians' context when I first heard the record. I remember looking at the pictures on the album cover and liking (and probably identifying with) the way that the women in the band looked. *Secondhand news, Don't stop* and *I don't want to know* played over and over again in my head. The words and the music seemed to be soaked in interpersonal anguish and I tried to recall how I had read the meaning of the lyrics back in 1977.

12 August 1997, Palm Springs.—More cable channel grazing brought me to a repeat showing of the *Classic Albums* programme. I saw a bit more of the story this time around, but still missed the start of the plot. The story of *Rumours* is that the five members of the band were in the midst of separation, divorce and acrimony – not to mention drugs, success and money. The songs on the album chart the bitterness and conflict and occasionally hint at better times to follow.

Uncovering truth, lies and Rumours

As the programme revealed, the record was made at a time when members of Fleetwood Mac were going through their own personal traumas. Stevie Nicks, one of the singer-songwriters in the band, was splitting from Lindsey Buckingham, lead guitarist and songwriter. Christine McVie, the third of the group's songwriters and the keyboard player, was getting divorced from bass player John McVie. Drummer Mick Fleetwood's marriage had also broken down, and his wife was having an affair with one of his friends. The album took a year to complete, and through much of it the five musicians were incarcerated together in the cultural island of the recording studio, in intense working relationships with, and close physical proximity to the partners with whom they were painfully breaking up. The hedonism and excess of the lifestyles of that period were remarked upon in several of the interviews, and many aspects of the *zeitgeist* as described in the recollections of Sausalito (where *Rumours* was recorded) seemed to parallel the style of my less affluent social circle in Leicester.

The summer of 1997 turned out to contain more media representations of Fleetwood Mac; after the *Rumours* programme there was a trailer for the cable television premiere of *The Dance*, Bruce Gowers' production featuring a reassembled Fleetwood Mac with the 1977 line-up. I scheduled my holiday viewing accordingly.

> *17 August 1997, Palm Springs.*—Watched *The Dance*, the television recording of Fleetwood Mac's 1997 reunion concert on VH1 (for the second time this week). I enjoyed the contemporary reworkings of the songs from *Rumours*, which were accompanied by some onstage re-enactment of the soap opera of the band's interpersonal relationships. I sat in bed drinking myself into a pleasant haze with Bacardi and Diet Coke, wept my way through half a box of Kleenex, and had a thoroughly happy time.

This indulgence in nostalgia seemed a slightly shameful pleasure, and it was one I found difficult to articulate and to explain to Rod, my partner, with whom I shared my Californian holiday. He is sufficiently older than me to have had quite different subcultural experiences. I construct him as having more theoretical knowledge of music than I have, because he once made a television series about opera, and I am gratified that he confirms *Rumours* to have musical merit and high production values. However, his skin responses to *Don't stop* or *I don't want to know* are clearly different from mine.

Researching representations of the goddess

I had spent so much time in California humming *Rumours* tracks that I wanted to flesh out this fragment of experience with some more research data. I dug in my personal archives for photographs of myself and my contemporaries during the *Rumours* era. I consulted *Rock Family Trees* to check on the band's musical genealogy, and confirmed my impression that Christine McVie (*née* Perfect) had once played in a West Midlands-based band called Chicken Shack. I was at school with a sister of one of Chicken Shack's guitarists. Somehow this small worlds connection seemed to help to render my visceral response to some elements in the music more susceptible to sociological analysis. Objects and icons which connect me now (a relatively affluent and moderately successful academic, living in London and working to maintain a still stylish and dangerous presence) to me then (a working-class grammar-school girl with false fingernails, a

Kidderminster accent and dreams of being famous) are sources of energy and excitement. I used to identify with cool blonde rock chicks and I guess a part of me still does. It seems a small step from the cool blonde rock chickdom of Perfect (a much better name than that of her husband, I should have thought) and Nicks to the mystical figure of the goddess, an archetype which both Stevie and Christine still weave with confidence into their narratives and performances.

Over the next six months I continued to collect as much data as I could find to help me make sense of the intersections of history, memory and affect with rock music. In true academic fashion, I reviewed relevant literature. I began with a narrow focus on Fleetwood Mac, first in their mid-70s constellation and later to line-ups before and after. After searches in bookshops and libraries across at least two continents (as well as on the Internet), I amassed a sizeable collection of autobiographical and hagiographical texts. Web searches took me through many a fanzine site and I lingered for several evenings among the archive of interviews from *Rolling Stone*. At the same time I collected as much audio-visual material as possible. I bought the CD and video of *The Dance* (which I had already recorded off-air), and a day or two later, I read a newspaper report that *The Dance* (released in the US two weeks earlier) had reached the top of the American rock charts. It seemed that the bit of intense personal experience I had in California, which had provoked my act of consumption shortly after, must have had parallels in a million lives.

I then set out to acquire on CD the entire back catalogue of Fleetwood Mac recordings, most of which I already owned on vinyl. Even if my 33s had survived the post-divorce division of marital property, I was unsure where to locate them, and, in any case, I had no turntable set up to play records anymore. But there were at least five CD players in the house. A boxed set of cassette tapes of Fleetwood Mac concerts and studio sessions which I found remaindered in a mall in Commerce, Georgia, afforded me many hours of pleasure in my car, the only place where I interact with magnetic tape music technology.

Through the long winter evenings of 1997, my quest to colonise my past and present selves, to chart new parts of my sociological and psychic imagination and to track their manifestations in musical rhythms and stories continued. I extended my research territory to move backwards and forwards in the rock family trees, invisible colleges and mythic structures into which the performers and texts of *Rumours* were connected. Just before Christmas, in an orgy of consumption which was supposed to be centred on buying gifts for others, I acquired for myself seven old rock videos and five CDs of almost-forgotten favourites from the 1970s retro section of Tower Records.

Finding the feminine in rock music

Although it seems obvious now, I was not aware of the unusual gender line-up of Fleetwood Mac in the mid-70s. My consciousness of the output of girl bands went back at least to The Ronettes, of course, but, then, as with 1990s manifestations such as the Spice Girls, I could not see them carrying strong connotations of feminist action, since their mode of production seemed so rooted in the male-dominated political economy of the 1950s. There were then and are now many instances of individual rock, folk and pop divas who have no doubt provided the stuff of self-fulfilment fantasies for many a young female, but single artistes of any gender have never appealed to me as much as performers who operate with balance and deftness in ensemble configurations. Christine McVie and Stevie Nicks are unusual amongst female rock performers in the companionable and creative sisterhood which is suggested in the close harmonies of their many recorded performances. Between them they have also written most of the band's most successful songs. Such women have to have a good deal of the goddess archetype about them. Some of the glamorous, dangerous elements of the rock goddess evident in Stevie Nicks's persona as constructed in the media were summed up concisely in an interview to which I made reference in a diary entry towards the end of my concentrated empirical activity for the technobiographies project:

12 February 1998, London.—*The Guardian* featured an interview with Stevie Nicks today. The article carried the strapline 'from seventies icon to nineties icon'. The interview notes that 'in her 49 years she has embodied every girl's fantasy of decadent rock'n'roll life, surviving affairs with two band members and an addiction to cocaine that cost her millions.'

I felt strangely satisfied that Nicks was back making headlines; it was as if I'd rediscovered her myself, back in the cable-delivered hyperreality of Palm Springs. At the same time, I was a little uneasy at the prospect of my private cult turning out to be congruent with mass taste. I jotted down a couple of items of evidence early in 1998 with a degree of gloom:

24 January 1998, London.—*Rumours* ranks no 23 in Channel Four's *Music of the Millennium.*

8 February 1998, London.—There's a massive Fleetwood Mac poster over Old Street roundabout. Last week they were given a lifetime achievement award at the Brits contemporary music awards.

Following the Brits ceremony, one close friend observed that while he found my analyses of contemporary cultural movements to have some merit, he was surprised at my choice of a special subject, since he saw Fleetwood Mac as too close to the mainstream to appeal to the subculturally discerning. I defended my interests by recourse to feminist ontology, epistemology and iconography as personified in Perfect-McVie and Nicks, but I was already starting to feel the need to extend my range of goddesses. When this particular friend visits these days, I feel impelled to bolster my hipness quotient by treating him to the obscurer corners of my CD collection. When I was reminded that Bill Clinton chose the Mac track *Don't stop (thinking about tomorrow)* as his presidential victory theme tune, I decided (a) that C.Wright Mills (1970) got it so right in showing the links between biography and history and (b) that perhaps I should like to shift my exploration and analysis to other elements in the zeitgeist.

Ending up closer to the goddess than the cyborg

Back in my cyborg's lair in late January 2001, I review the significance of all these travels in time, over continents, through cyberspace and memory. I replay conversations in my head and on the disks and those made possible by train, plane, telephone, fax, tape, post and email.

My technobiographical narrative has focused on some case studies of the significance of technological objects and processes in my life history. From the specific examples of the technologies of plumbing and music reproduction I have attempted to highlight how the relations of class, gender, generation and subculture have helped to shape the objects in question and are at the same time symbolically inscribed on their surfaces and properties. Many of the objects with which I interact daily also have aspects of my identity stamped on them.

While I have described individual and hitherto private feelings, I assume that others will identify with some patterns in my story. Contemporary media technologies are constantly recycling individual and collective memory and experience – not to mention old programmes and out-takes – in the desperate search for content to fill up the time and space created by new channels and greater bandwidth.

If what Haraway's cyborg metaphor is supposed to offer is a way of transcending boundaries and changing identities, then for me goddess does it better. Probably the issue of generation, which emerges as a major theme in my internal drama, has relevance to my preference. If I was a sexy young woman in the 1970s – a hippie rock chick flirting with utopian social movements and eschewing aspects of technology – then I was also a child of the 1950s, devouring American sci-fi comics where the metallic creatures which are conjured up in the word cyborg were always the baddies. In 1990, Johnny Depp gave the protagonist of Tim Burton's film *Edward Scissorhands* a certain charm as a creature who was part-man, part-cutlery drawer, but a romantic object who had always to be kept at more than arm's length would provide limited satisfaction in one of my internal narratives.

It was easy to assert my preference to be a goddess rather than a cyborg when I began to write this chapter. I was influenced by my personal experience and my irritation with what I confess I read as Haraway's frequently leaden prose. Her manifesto is alleged to be written in a spirit of irony, but I find it hard to find anything in it to make me smile, let alone giggle. And I should want to argue for the retention of at least some qualities of what used in post-structuralist language to be termed the fully-constituted human subject. At the same time, I cannot deny that there are touches of the cyborg in my identity, revealed in the hardware which surrounds me as I write, and the software which enables me to revisit earlier selves and sensations.

Nevertheless, if I am faced with a forced choice along the lines of 'be a cyborg or goddess or die', then I must opt for goddess every time. The archetype of the magical mysterious figure of the powerful, beautiful superhuman female (embodied in modern times as the glamorous actress or rock singer) is much more magnetic than the shiny techno-subject, and more fun to cast and play in my technobiographical narrative. Goddesses seem to me to have many of the characteristics which are alleged to represent advantages in the cyborg metaphor: goddesses cross boundaries between the human and the superhuman, the powerful and the vulnerable, the social and the natural world. They can be shapeshifters, mentors or guardians, awesome allies or formidable foes. The goddess is a creature I should like to emulate, as well as to have on my side throughout my technobiographical journey. A part of me is fixed forever as a blonde (but not dumb) rock chick, more goddess than cyborg.

Acknowledgements

Thanks again to all those in my technobiographical invisible college who helped with the story of this chapter. You are all in here somewhere. I've named as many as seemed decent in the Acknowledgements to this book. I am sorry that my dad is not alive to read and argue about the visits to Wilson's. My co-editors have earned my undying affection through their patience, tact and sisterhood; thank you (in strict alphabetical order), Flis and Helen.

Bibliography

Bell, D. and Kennedy, B.M. (eds) (2000) *The Cybercultures Reader*, London: Routledge.

Berne, E. (1973) *What do you say after you say hello?* New York: Bantam Books.

Bijker, W.E. (1993) 'Do not despair: There is life after constructivism', *Science, Technology & Human Values* 18, 1: 113-38.

Boud, D. and Miller, N. (eds) (1996) *Working with experience: animating learning.* London: Routledge.

Caldicott, H. (1996) *A Desperate Passion: An Autobiography*, New York: Norton.

Cherny, L. and Weise, E.R. (eds) (1996) *Wired Women: Gender and New Realities in Cyberspace*, Washington: Seal Press.

Clare, M. and Johnson, R. (2000) 'Method in our madness? Identity and power in a memory work method', in S. Radstone (ed.) *Memory and Methodology*, New York and Oxford: Berg.

Cockburn, C. and Ormrod, S. (1993) *Gender and Technology in the Making*, London: Sage.

Coupland, D. (1996) *Microserfs*. London: Flamingo.

Coyle, K. (1996) 'How Hard Can It Be?' in L. Cherny and E.R. Weise (eds) *Wired Women: Gender and New Realities in Cyberspace*, Washington: Seal Press.

Davis-Floyd, R. and Dumit, J. (eds) (1998) *Cyborg Babies: From Techno-Sex to Techno-Tots*, London: Routledge.

DP Connect (1997) *Women in IT Campaign Brief*, Bromley: DP Connect.

Dvorak, J. (1995) 'DOS is Alive, and Well ...' *PC Magazine*, 13 December.

Edge, D. (1995) 'Reinventing the wheel', in S. Jasanoff, G.E. Markle, J.C.

Petersen & T. Pinch (eds) *Handbook of Science and Technology Studies*, London: Sage.

Ellul, J. (1954) *The Technological Society*, New York: Random House (orig. *La Technique ou l'Enjeu du Siècle*, 1954).

Graham, E. (1999) 'Cyborgs or goddesses? Becoming divine in a cyberfeminist age', *Information, Communication & Society* 2, 4: 419-38.

Gray, C.H. (1995) (ed.) *The Cyborg Handbook*, New York: Routledge.

Grint, K. and Gill, R. (eds) (1995) *The Gender-Technology Relation: Contemporary Theory and Research*, London: Taylor & Francis.

Hall, S., Held, D. and McGrew, T. (eds) (1992) *Modernity and its Futures*, Oxford: Polity Press in association with the Open University.

Haraway, D. (1985) 'A manifesto for cyborgs: Science, technology and socialist feminism in the 1980s', *Socialist Review*, 80: 65–107.

Haraway, D. (1991) *Simians, Cyborgs and Women: The Reinvention of Nature*, London: Free Association Books.

Harrison, D. (1988) *The Sociology of Modernization and Development*, London: Unwin Hyman.

Haug, F. and others (1987) *Female Sexualization: A Collective Work of Memory*, trans. E. Carter, London: Verso.

Hebdige, D. (1979) *Subculture: The Meaning of Style*, London: Routledge.

Hollway, W. (1989) *Subjectivity and Method in Psychology: Gender, Meaning and Science*, London: Sage.

Johnson, F. (1996) 'Cyberpunks in the White House' in J. Dovey (ed.) *Fractal Dreams: New Media in Social Context*, London: Lawrence and Wishart.

Johnson, R. (1997) 'Contested borders, contingent lives' in D.L. Steinberg, D. Epstein and R. Johnson (eds) *Border Patrols: Policing the Boundaries of Heterosexuality*, London: Cassell.

Kelly, A. (1987), *Science for Girls*, Milton Keynes: Open University Press.

Kennedy, H. (1999) 'Identity construction in a virtual world: The homepage as auto/biographical practice', *Auto/Biography* 7, 1 & 2: 91-8.

Kennedy, H., Leung, L. and Miller, N. (2000) 'Project @THENE: Widening access in virtual learning communities' in T. Butler (ed.) *Eastern Promise: Education and Social Renewal in London's Docklands*, London: Lawrence and Wishart.

Kirkup, G. (2000) 'Introduction to Part One', in G. Kirkup, L. James, K. Woodward and F. Hovenden (eds) *The Gendered Cyborg*, London: Routledge.

Kirkup, G., James, L., Woodward, K. and Hovenden, F. (eds) (2000) *The Gendered Cyborg*, London: Routledge.

Kuhn, T. (1962) *The Structure of Scientific Revolutions*, Chicago, IL: University of Chicago Press.

Latour, B. (1986) 'Visualisation and cognition: Thinking with eyes and hands', *Knowledge and Society: Studies in the Sociology of Culture Past and Present* 6: 1-40.

Latour, B. (1992) 'Where are the missing masses? The sociology of a few mundane artefacts', in W. Bijker and J. Law (eds) *Shaping Technology/ Building Society, Studies in Sociotechnical Change*, Cambridge, MA: MIT Press.

Latour, B. (1996) *Aramis or the Love of Technology*, trans. C. Porter, Cambridge, MA: Harvard University Press.

Latour, B. and Woolgar, S. (1979) *Laboratory Life: The Social Construction of Scientific Facts*, (2nd edition) Princeton, NJ: Princeton University Press.

Law, J. (2000) 'On the subject of the object: Narrative, technology, and interpellation', *Configurations* 8, 1: 1-29.

Lee, P. (1991) 'The Absorption of Foreign Media Culture', *Asian Journal of Communication* 1, 2: 52-72.

Levy, S. (1994) *Insanely Great: The Life and Times of the Macintosh, the Computer that Changed Everything*, New York: Penguin Books.

Liddle, J. and Joshi, R. (1988) *Daughters of Independence: Gender, Caste and Class in India*, London: Zed Press.

Lie, M. and Sørenson, K.H. (eds) (1996) *Making Technology Our Own? Domesticating Technology into Everyday Life*, Oslo: Scandinavian University Press.

Lippard, L. (1992) 'Mapping' in F. Frascina and J. Harris (eds) *Art in Modern Culture*, London: Phaidon Press.

Lykke, N. (1996) 'Between monsters, goddesses and cyborgs: Feminist confrontations with science', in N. Lykke and R. Braidotti (eds) *Between Monsters, Goddesses and Cyborgs: Feminist Confrontations with Science, Medicine and Cyberspace*, London: Zed Press.

Lykke, N. and Braidotti, R. (eds) (1996) *Between Monsters, Goddesses and Cyborgs: Feminist Confrontations with Science, Medicine and Cyberspace*, London: Zed Press.

MacKenzie, D. and Wajcman, J. (eds) (1985) *The Social Shaping of Technology*, Milton Keynes: Open University Press.

Miller, N. (1993a) 'Doing adult education research through autobiography' in N. Miller and D. Jones (eds) *Research: Reflecting Practice: papers from the 1993 SCUTREA Conference*, Boston: SCUTREA, 88-92.

Miller, N. (1993b) *Personal experience, social research and adult learning: developing a sociological imagination in and beyond the T-group*, Adelaide: University of South Australia.

Miller, N. (2000) 'Lifelong learning goes to the movies: autobiographical narratives as media production' in Sork, T., Chapman, V.-L. and St. Clair, R. (eds) *Proceedings of the 41st Annual Adult Education Research Conference (AERC)*, Vancouver: University of British Columbia, 267–273.

Miller, N. and Morgan, D. (1992) 'Called to account: the CV as an autobiographical practice', *Sociology* 27, 1: 133-43.

Mills, C. W. (1970) *The Sociological Imagination*, Harmondsworth: Penguin (first published 1959).

Misa, T. (1988) 'How machines make history, and how historians (and others) help them to do so', *Science, Technology and Human Values* 13, 3 & 4: 308-31.

Morley, D. and Robins, K. (1995) 'Culture, community and identity: communications technologies and the reconfiguration of Europe' in D. Morley and K. Robins (eds) *Spaces of Identity: Global Media, Electronic Landscapes and Cultural Boundaries*, London: Routledge.

Mumford, L. (1967) *The Myth of the Machine*, New York: Harcourt, Brace, Jovanovich.

Plant, S. (1997) *Zeros + Ones: Digital Women and the New Technoculture*, London: Fourth Estate.

Rapp, R. (1988) 'Chromosomes and communication: the discourse of genetic counseling', *Medical Anthropology Quarterly* 2: 143-157.

Rapp, R. (1993) 'Accounting for amniocentesis', in S. Lindenbaum and M. Lock (eds) *Knowledge, Power and Practice: The Anthropology of Medicine and Everyday Life*, Berkeley: University of California Press.

Rapp, R. (1998) 'Refusing prenatal diagnosis: the meanings of bioscience in a multicultural world', *Science, Technology and Human Values*, 23, 1: 45-70.

Reich, C. (1971) *The Greening of America*, New York: Bantam.

Roberts, H. (ed) (1981) *Doing Feminist Research*, London: Routledge and Kegan Paul.

Rose, H. (1994) *Love, Power and Knowledge: Towards a Feminist Transformation of the Sciences*, Cambridge: Polity.

Rothman, B.K. (1986) *Tentative Pregnancy: Prenatal Diagnosis and the Future of*

Motherhood, New York: Viking.

Rothschild, J. (ed) (1983) *Machina Ex Dea: Feminist Perspectives on Technology*, New York: Pergamon.

Saetnan, A.R. (1996) 'Speaking of gender ... intertwinings of a medical technology policy debate and everyday life', in M. Lie and K.H. Sørensen (eds) *Making Technology Our Own: Domesticating Technology into Everyday Life*, Oslo: Scandinavian University Press.

Said, E. (1992) 'Orientalism' in F. Frascina and J. Harris (eds) *Art in Modern Culture*, London: Phaidon Press.

Sayre, A. (1975) *Rosalind Franklin and DNA*, New York: Norton.

Sigurdsson, S. (1997) 'Electric memories and progressive forgetting', in T. Söderqvist (ed.) *The Historiography of Contemporary Science and Technology*, Amsterdam: Harwood.

Silverstone, R. and Hirsch, E. (eds) (1992) *Consuming Technologies: Media and Information in Domestic Spaces*, London: Routledge.

Singhal, A. and Rogers, E.M. (1989) *India's Information Revolution*, London: Sage.

Snow, C.P. (1993) The Two Cultures. Cambridge: Cambridge University Press (first published in 1959).

Spilker, H. and Sørensen, K.H. (2000) 'A ROM of one's own or a home for sharing? Designing the inclusion of women in multimedia', *New Media & Society* 2, 3: 268-84.

Squires, J. (1996) 'Fabulous feminist futures and the lure of cyberculture', in J. Dovey (ed.) *Fractal Dreams: New Media in Social Context*, London: Lawrence and Wishart.

Stanley, L. (1992) *The Auto/Biographical I: The Theory and Practice of Feminist Auto/Biography*, Manchester: Manchester University Press.

Stanley, L. (1990) *Feminist Praxis: Research, Theory and Epistemology in Feminist Sociology*, London: Routledge.

Star, S.L. (1991) 'Power, technologies and the phenomenology of conventions: on being allergic to onions', in J. Law (ed) *A Sociology of Monsters, Essays on Power, Technology and Domination*, London: Routledge.

Steedman, C. (1987) *Landscape for a Good Woman: A Story of Two Lives*, London: Virago.

Stephenson, N. (2000) *Cryptonomicon*, London: Arrow Books.

Subrahmanyan, L. (1998) *Women Scientists in the Third World: the Indian Experience*, London: Sage.

Swindells, J. (ed.) (1995) *The Uses of Autobiography*, London: Taylor & Francis.

The Shorter Oxford English Dictionary (1983) London: Guild Publishing.

Traweek, S. (1988) *Beamtimes and Lifetimes: The World of High Energy Physicists*, Cambridge, MA: Harvard University Press.

Ullman, E. (1996) 'Come in CQ: the body on the wire', in L. Cherny and E. R.Weise (eds) *Wired Women: Gender and New Realities in Cyberspace*, Washington: Seal Press.

van der Ploeg, I. and van Wingerden, I. (1995) 'Celebrating the cyborg? On the fate of a beautiful metaphor in later users' hands', *The European Journal of Women's Studies* 2: 397-400.

Vogler, C. (1996) *The writer's journey: mythic structure for storytellers and screenwriters* (revised edition), London: Boxtree.

Walkerdine, V. (1989) *Democracy in the Kitchen*, London: Virago.

Weise, E.R. (1996) 'A thousand aunts with modems', in L. Cherny and E.R. Weise (eds) *Wired Women: Gender and New Realities in Cyberspace*, Washington: Seal Press.

Winner, L. (1977) *Autonomous Technology, Technics-out-of-Control as a Theme in Political Thought*, Cambridge, MA: MIT Press.

Wittig, M. (1997) 'One is not born a woman' in S. Kemp and J. Squires (eds) *Feminisms*, Oxford: Oxford University Press.

Wolmark, J. (ed) (1999) *Cybersexualities: A Reader in Feminist Theory, Cyborgs and Cyberspace*, Edinburgh: Edinburgh University Press.

Women Working Worldwide (eds) (1991) *Common Interests: Women Organising in Global Electronics*, London: Women Working Worldwide.

Wyatt, A. (1978) *The Nuclear Challenge: Understanding The Debate*, Toronto: The Book Press.

Wyatt, R. (1977) *The Rosedale Hoax*, Toronto: Anansi Press.

Wyatt, S. (1998) *Technology's Arrow, Developing Information Networks for Public Administration in Britain and the United States*, Maastricht: University Pers Maastricht.

Wyatt, S., Henwood, F., Miller, N. and Senker, P. (eds) (2000) *Technology and In/equality, Questioning the Information Society*, London: Routledge.

Digital references

Australian Chinese Museum. Online (1998) 'Paintings by Eu-Huang (Christina) Chung' at http://www.cs.mu.oz.au/~lyk/exhibit/exhibit.html. 27 January 2001.

Chan, M. (1997) 'What Confucius didn't say' in *China City: bringing an Asian Canadian community to you* at http://www.asian.ca/media/chinacity/confu.htm.

Johansson, P. (1997) 'Consuming the Other: Representations of Western Women in Chinese Women's Advertising' in Paper proposal for the AAS Annual Meeting at http://orient4.orient.su.se/chinese/perry/chicago.htm. 13 March 2000.

Multimedia Production Centre, University of East London (2000) *Knowledge Dock: new landscapes*, CD-rom, London: Xor.

National Film Board of Canada Online (1998) 'Chinese Canadians' at http://www.nfb.ca/FMT/E/MSN/17/17806.html. 8 January 2001.

Ryan, J. (1996) 'Chinese in Australia: challenging the generalisations' in *Quest* at http://www.ecuinfo.cowan.edu.au/ecuwis/docs/res/quest/mar96.html. Volume 4, Number 1. March 2000.

Shirley and Terry (1997) 'Cross cultural marriages' at http://www.ibride.com/ibride/meetings/etiqroom/276.html. 6 April 2000.

Tobin, J. (1998). Online. 'Jason J Tobin' at http://www.momentum-hk.com/jason/intro.html. 28 January 2001.

Index